Beyond Conception: Our Children's Children

Beyond Conception: Our Children's Children

Martha Kent Willing

Gambit
INCORPORATED
Boston
1971

Excerpt on pages 202-203 from *The Essence of Christianity* by Ludwig Fueuerbach, translated from the German by George Eliot. Copyright © 1957 by Harper Brothers, Torchbooks; reprinted by permission of Harper & Row.
Excerpts on pages 205-206 from the *Introduction to St. Thomas Aquinas*, edited by Anton C. Pegis. Copyright © 1948 by Random House, Inc., Modern Library; reprinted by permission of Random House, Inc.

FIRST PRINTING

Library of Congress Catalog Card Number: 76-160416
Printed in the United States of America
ISBN 0-87645-044-3

to Elizabeth Cryer Kent

*who filled my childhood with
night skies and vivid places
and enjoyment of living things*

Acknowledgments

THIS BOOK is rooted in many deeply felt experiences: as an observer in the field, as a biologist in the laboratory, as a student of philosophy. But it came to be written only after several years of trying to explain population and birth control to women in clinics and to groups of students. I realized that most families in America are beyond the reach of clinic or college. They are busy raising children or supporting them. Yet they are an essential part of the population dilemma. I have tried to write a vivid, correct and simple book about very difficult ideas, some of which are far from popular. Lately, however, the public has been running far ahead in its attitudes toward pollution and the war. Unlike many of my colleagues in the field, I think population control will be accepted far more rapidly than we expect. The facts are just too obvious to be avoided.

In this place I want to thank Mary Summerfield Gardiner of Bryn Mawr College, and Thomas W. Edmondson of the University of Washington, for their rich vision of biology which they shared through many hours of valuable teaching time.

W. Siang Shu will recognize in what way his perceptive scholarship influenced this task.

The patience of my family, Shippen Willing and Steve, was only exceeded by the patience and exactitude of Mark Saxton, of Gambit. It was a happy circumstance which led me to his office.

My cheerful typists, Marlene Cook and Kareen Maschmann, will be relieved to see the final copy.

Most of all, thanks are due to George C. Denniston, MD. Without the opportunity to work in his clinics, without his wholehearted concern for population, I would not have written this book.

M.K.W.
Seattle, March 25, 1971

Contents

Preface

DURING A WYOMING VACATION in 1948 I read Fairfield Osborn's *Our Plundered Planet* and first became conscious of a population problem. I have become increasingly concerned ever since. This concern led me to respond to an invitation to attend a Planned Parenthood Committee Board meeting in my hometown of Pittsburgh in 1952. I recall entering the back door of the building with my hat pulled well down in the hope that I would remain unrecognized in those early years of the movement. I came away a staunch supporter.

As a trustee of a charitable foundation, I had recently voted for the construction and endowment of a Graduate School of Public Health at the University of Pittsburgh. Then came the slow realization that the population dilemma was being caused not by some sudden increase in human fertility but by the unrelenting application of death control by public health physicians and medical missionaries throughout the world, with no concurrent effort being devoted to the other side of the equation —birth control. The result was that death rates everywhere were being cut in half while birth rates remained level. It was not difficult to foresee that by thus upsetting the balance of nature for millions of people their misery was to be compounded instead of alleviated. Since Public Health, however, is broadly concerned with the total ecology, it has been encouraging to observe that the profession is now actively engaged in trying once again to reduce the birth rate everywhere to equate with the death rate.

In 1954 I met with Gen. Frederick Osborn, the first president of The Population Council, to learn of the organization's research activities in demography and physiology of reproduction. Founded by John D. Rockefeller III, The Population Council is possibly the outstanding act of philanthropy of the postwar years. In 1960 the Princeton meeting convened by Hugh Moore launched the World Population Emergency Campaign, which was the first attempt to raise larger funds from the business community. World Population was soon taken over by Planned Parenthood. In 1965, realizing that the problem had both domestically and internationally outgrown the resources and capabilities of private organizations, Hugh Moore once again called a meeting, in Washington, D.C., to found the Population Crisis Committee. Its purpose was to encourage government leaders to recognize the enormity and seriousness of the problem and take action in time to bring about population stabilization.

As a result of my involvement in these developments, I was called upon on two occasions to give testimony to my beliefs regarding population problems which would be in direct variance with the current views of my audience. The first was an address to a distinguished group of corporate executives in New York in 1962 under the auspices of Planned Parenthood—World Population, in which it became necessary to challenge the widely held thesis that continuing population growth was good for business. If numbers of people alone were important for sales, then Asia would be the greatest market on earth. This is not the case because only people with purchasing power make good customers, and purchasing power is a result of the standard of living and industrial productivity rather than the number of people. Thus Canada with 4% of India's population carries on a trade with the United States which is twenty times as great as that of India. I also pointed out that if United States Gross National Product since the end of World War II is corrected for inflation and the growth of population, the real per capita growth of GNP is only about 15% of the uncorrected figure —a not too impressive record. To the extent future sales increase is the result of population growth, there is a distinct likelihood that higher taxes will be levied on corporations to provide for accelerated welfare and social costs which will nullify much of the increase in the final net profit.

On the second occasion I was invited to address the annual meeting of the Planned Parenthood Federation in New York in November 1968. The thrust of my remarks was that the long-cherished position of Planned Parenthood in regard to family planning was not enough. The reason was that many couples do not begin to plan their families until they have already had four or more children (six to twelve in underdeveloped countries); if all couples of childbearing age have four children, the population automatically doubles in each generation of twenty-five years. In the decade prior to 1967, United States couples had been having 3.2 children. Since the caseload of the Planned Parenthood clinics in the principal cities of the United States did not reach 1% of the women of childbearing age, the problem of population growth was not the "unwanted child" of the 5,000,000 poor women, but the "wanted child" of the 45,000,000 other women of childbearing age. I suggested that the policy of Planned Parenthood be altered to include activities which would convince the leaders of government and citizen groups that they must devise motivational techniques which would literally change the mores and customs of the nation from the traditional one of large families to the modern requirement of small families.

The challenge to all will be whether we can develop the will and discipline to accomplish this by voluntary means alone or whether society for its own health and preservation must impose involuntary restraints.

Because of this background and evolution of thought in regard to the population problem, I commend to all readers this important new book by Martha Willing. It provides new insights and concepts which will be a worthy addition to the literature and which can be read with profit by both novice and expert. It is my hope that the book will provide youth with challenge and new purpose in abundance to substitute the goal of quality of life for quantity of life; my hope also is that the book will lead to accelerated action.

Adolph W. Schmidt, U.S. Ambassador to Canada
Ottawa, Canada, May 10, 1971

(The opinions expressed above by Mr. Schmidt are his own and not necessarily those of the Department of State.)

Prolog

ALL OVER THE WORLD we—the living—have produced too many children. Yet with the terrible bigotry of fixed societies, adults are excusing the status quo and putting off as long as possible the simple remedy of having none or one or two children.

Evidence is pouring in: from science and medicine, from agriculture and industry, but most alarmingly from the naturalists who come and tell us the fish are dead, there are no American eagles—where are the butterflies? The evidence implies that we must reverse population trends as fast as possible. We cannot remain frozen in shock, in old habits, in refusal to know, for if we do, we are condemning millions of children to be born; not at first to die but to live worse and worse. What was once a great good has become an appalling evil.

To react as though to tragedy is a mistake, for this problem is capable of pleasing solutions. Solving it promises more joy and greater human value than solving any other problem facing us. Far from leading to repression and dictatorship, smaller numbers of people and wiser use of resources are conditions underlying any freedom at all.

If we truly love children and not ourselves only, we will listen with care to the population story.

The Green Lung

1

THE EARTH has always seemed enormous and secure. Men explored its far lands with excitement, and spoke with comfort of the soil beneath their feet. Now the earth seems fragile and terribly small, floating in its wisps and streets of cloud cover. Beyond, the blue-black night looms hostile, infinitely extended, cold, without pressure of oxygen for survival. Only on the surface of the sphere are there conditions for simple unprotected life.

We may think of a globe as something we fill. But this globe, the earth, is not a hollow containing life: it is a thin shell between molten rock and freezing atmosphere, a sun-trap, each day capturing energy, warming and breathing with it, each night resting and cooling, a synchronous turning in space of the thinnest envelope where living creatures, plant and animal, make the most insignificant of films between impossible conditions.

The greenery of the earth's surface is the breathing green lung of this film. Active in the sunlight, the breathing compounds of the green leaf take in carbon dioxide and give off oxygen. This essential exchange between plants and the atmosphere made the first animals a possibility. Oxygen in the atmosphere never seems to be replenished except through this set of light-sensitive compounds, the chlorophylls and xanthophylls found in leaves, algae, diatoms and lichens. Carbon dioxide in the atmosphere came first, then the plants, and only as oxygen increased were the oxidizing animal compounds able to begin their history.

The green film grew up from thin diatoms and lichens to mighty tree ferns in the carboniferous and, as temperatures fell, were displaced by the northern evergreens. Only recently these evergreen forests dominated the landscape between latitudes 45 to 65 degrees across Europe, North America and vast stretches of Siberia. Green forests clothed the tropics with luxuriant layer upon layer of sophisticated sun-traps, leaves graded to capture and use in living tissue even the dim filtered light of the tropical forest floor. Abundance of plants, abundance of rapidly developing oxygen breathers, creeping, crawling, flying, learning to walk at first on all fours, then upright, in the luxury and protection of the green film!

Standing anywhere on the green floor, either on the wide grasslands, in the fern forests, in the northern taiga, man surveys an environment which looks empty, spacious, inexhaustible. The food, warmth, shelter and trade of human affairs have been hewed and hauled out of this same green film. The animal kingdom increased at the expense of the green breathers of carbon dioxide. But this is not apparent to any of the creatures surveying their world. The living eye, intent upon survival in the green film, must accept its present vision as eternal, as truth telling. Watchful, endangered, the eye itself has no perception backward in time, nor outward beyond a little distance. By looking it gleans no suspicion of its history.

Human beings contained within their environment might have roamed an area of several hundred miles in a lifetime. Some, taking to the seas or to caravan roamed farther. But the vast majority of human creatures move in a narrow circle of trade and feeding even today. Each farmer, burning down and bulldozing over a field, is unaware of how many other farmers are doing the same thing. Lumber companies compare profits and markets, but do not compare the ultimate green lung they are collectively cutting and melting down into containers, paper pulp, building materials. Only from the highest atmosphere can the steady thinning and retreat of the green film be charted by an observing eye.

Science, the dry mathematicizing of vital events, is our only source of surveillance of ourselves. By the methods of science we can measure the loss of leaf surface, the rise of oxygen consumption by animals, the competing carbon dioxide put out by every form of energy conversion. Carbon dioxide plumes forth from factory chimneys, from the tailpipes of cars and the exhaust of outboards. It fumes behind Hondas and spews from smelters and hospitals and newborn little lungs which come squalling into the world at the rate of three a second. Production of carbon dioxide, consumption of oxygen, these are the basic theorems of human life. Where is their ultimate balance, where is the danger point?

The ground beneath our feet can be delved into at great energy-expense, but will yield us only fractional additional living space. We are building up, twenty stories, fifty stories, one hundred stories; we are moving up the slopes of mountains and out onto the edges of the desert; and we are extending our notions of living space into and under the sea. But each such extension from the natural primitive habitations of men costs a vast outlay in energy per man.

The latest development in energy comes from atomic fuels. The supply is so vast it seems inexhaustible. We are beginning to heat and light America by means of these energies. Other countries will follow. These energies are smokeless, noiseless, clean—and deadly. Where will we place the by-products of atomic power? Burying them in the ground is proving dangerous: the cement kegs crack and leak into the ground water. When oceanographers probed the deep ocean looking for a disposal site they found that the ocean deep-currents are part of a vast slow recirculation which replenishes the nutrients of the green layers of the sea. Testing fallout in the Pacific islands we found that many marine animals concentrate "hot" ions in their body structure far in excess of the tiny amounts in the surrounding water. Thus we are placing this poison not only into the air we breathe, but randomly into the food chains of all fish-eating peoples. Animals concentrate tiny amounts of dangerous ions. We are animals. What are we about to do to ourselves? No one is able to tell us.

In addition to the "hot" ions which disrupt the cellular integrity of life, we have a serious problem of heat. Steady release of energy in the form of heat must accompany the production of electric power, whether produced from atomic or from fossil fuels. Already water from atomic heat-exchangers is altering the ecosystems of Long Island Sound and Lake Ontario.

A slow warming of the atmosphere seems to have occurred before in geologic history. Right now, the evidence for continental drift leaves us unsure whether the north pole was once located at some other point on the earth's surface, or whether the continents now bordering the Arctic Ocean drifted there from much more tropical seas. We are sure, however, that the climate of the earth has been, on the average, both some degrees colder and some degrees warmer than it is right now. These balances are narrow, and recorded fluctuations of the mean seem very narrow to have caused such tremendous changes as the ice invasions of the recent geologic past. Significant human intervention in the temperature cycles of the world has come about only in the last fifty years with the growth of population and the enormous demand for energy to support this population. In all energy conversions the loss escapes into the ecosphere as heat. Natural man shudders at the large vagaries of climate; the scientific mind ponders dubiously the risk of even a slight rise in the temperature mean.

The green shell, poised between hot rock and cold space is confined to a rim no more than three habitable miles thick, from the Dead Sea, to the passes of the Himalayas. North and south it is covered with thermostatic icecaps. Everywhere it is interspersed with water; relatively shallow seas covering three-fifths of the surface of the sphere. This living shell is the container of the total human population. This thin layer is our prison, from which only at the cost of enormous and special energy not open to the crowd can a few escape for a moment into space or under ocean. Here we shall carry on the wild overproduction and dying-off of unstable populations, or we shall come to an equilibrium among ourselves and with the energy budgets which control the ultimate balance between green lung of the plant kingdom and flexing muscle of animals.

Balance

2

How CAN a population be in balance? What sort of balance do we mean and how do we examine into it? Recent developments in animal studies suggest some clues. The choicest summer real estate of isolated lakes and rivers is the breeding territory of the northern loon. One of our largest, most primitive birds, loons are surviving due to ancient balances. In the northern forest, if we were to walk before daybreak down a path to the water's edge, we might be lucky enough to see them.

At the water's edge, we shiver. Fog collects and runs delicately into the shallows from the tips of willow and fir. The pearl-gray surface of the lake smokes with early mist. Daybreak songs spill from overhanging branches of birch and hemlock. Suddenly a fast-moving ripple silvers the point. A large bird lashes the water with wings and feet, attempting and failing to fly. Then with great poise he sweeps slowly to a halt, turns easily and dives. He surfaces, shakes, looks around and dives suddenly again, this time surfacing close in by the hemlocks. There, swimming quietly along the shore the female loon and two downy young join him. The adults preen and circle. The little ones disappear. Then the old birds begin to swim rapidly across the arm of the lake. Tiny heads poke out securely from the angle between parent wing and body feathers. Comical, touching, serene, the babies are ferried to the day's fishing ground.

In August the old birds finish the moult which has kept

them powerless to fly until the young can also leave the water. Then the family moves off on those late-season wanderings common to most northern waterbirds. On stormy nights the cry of the loon rings overhead.

This wild lake is several irregular miles around with many small islands. Year after year one pair of loons, perhaps not the same pair, flies in soon after the ice breaks in the spring. Each year the great birds raise one or two young loons. A young bird must eat constantly to grow and maintain a body temperature several degrees higher than a man's. Loons are voracious feeders, mainly on fish. The supply of minnows must not become reduced in the lake or the supply of loons would disappear from it. This handsome, seemingly untameable bird each year does tame his habits to a tiny horizon of water and food supply. While loons on their nesting grounds are almost always found in solitary pairs, in winter they are still abundant off the New England and Pacific coastal bays, and seem in no present danger of extinction. How do they manage to limit and yet maintain a population? We do not know.

The average loon, like man, has chiefly man to fear. He defends nest territory, feeds and teaches the young until the fall departure. But the young never come back to the lake of their origin when the old birds return in the spring. Where do they go, near or far? Did they live through the winter, or is this pair the young of several years ago, now undetectably replacing their parents who have disappeared? These are questions in process of study. The key fact remains to baffle us: there are still loons, and there are never too many of them.

The human family lives in kinship or tribal units which seem to have definite advantages over the solitary breeding pair. Communal food-getting, child-rearing and defense of the home territory have made us into "social" animals. But only partially so. To locate ourselves in the spectrum of social behavior, we need to consider not only the solitary breeding pair of loons, but highly organized social insects like the honeybees.

Powerful instincts motivate the honeybee to maintain integrity of the hive at all costs, including instant sacrifice of the individual. The stinging bee, a female nonsexual worker can sting but once and dies. Her weapon is her death warrant. Yet when the angry hive roars out in defense the mass suicide is instant and can be afforded because these defenders are not the reproducers of the hive.

The hive has built-in population controls to deal with the two essential shortages of space and of food. The bees respond to the heavy fruit and flower bloom of early spring. One can watch them tumbling over the yellow and orange stamens of the crocus and hear the purring of an apple tree in full blossom whenever the sun, shining down, provides the critical level of warmth for the bee-wing to function and the hive to harvest nectar and pollen. Even though rainy weeks and scant flow of nectar usually follow the spring flow, larvae are hatching and the young bees are crowding the comb, because the early flow sets off rapid egg-laying and bee-rearing. The interior of the hive becomes congested. On a warm day, one can hear the music of the hive step up its volume of wings. Crowding becomes evident. Something in this combination causes the nurse bees to feed certain young larvae a special hormone jelly which turns them into new, fertile queens. Just before the new queens hatch from their enlarged cells, the old queen and the field-working bees swarm from the hive. This usually occurs on a sunny morning, and the swarm flies excitedly in the sunshine. The queen alights on a shrub or tree nearby. The flying bees settle around her hanging in a cluster. Scout bees meanwhile have located a new nest in a house wall or in a hollow tree, and after some delay and elaborate dancing, the adult swarm streaks off in a dark roaring column to this new place. There, new comb-building and egg-laying will begin. The old hive has space once again.

This mass migration occurs in the northern states just before the main nectar flows. The honey crop differs from one region

to another. In some of the western plains of America it is alfalfa, or seed clover; in the east it is often a tree from the forest
edge, the locust, the basswood, the tulip poplar, or field buck-
wheat; in some areas it is the tiny white clover of lawns and
pastures.

While the deserted hive is busy developing new field bees,
while the virgin queen goes on her mating flight and returns to
a life of egg-laying to replenish the population, the departed
swarm of mature bees is foraging madly and building comb to
make a new brood chamber for the old queen. Such a swarm
builds new comb in hot weather with maximum efficiency.

These are the essential population responses of the hive
which have been diverted by beekeepers to their own use—
sometimes to provide fresh combs, sometimes to prevent
swarming so that surplus honey shall be maximized, sometimes
to rear many young hybrid queens for sale, sometimes to produce maximum pounds of young field bees to lease for pollina-
tion to commercial growers of alfalfa or orchards. These responses permit the docile honeybee to produce many
thousands of times more honey or more bees than it needs in
nature. But the natural response of the bees to ample food supply is rapid build-up of population and mass migration.

For bees, there is another population response every year.
After the summer honey flow, when food is scarce, egg-laying
drops off. The tempo of life in the hive changes. Days are
shorter. Nights begin to be cool. Instead of rapid coming and
going, traffic at the doorstep of the hive is slower. There are
more bystanders fanning their wings or walking slowly. The
worker bees now have to fly further afield and many of them
are lost on the way back. The male drones which were produced abundantly in the spring to fertilize the new queens
have been tolerated through the flush months, personally fed
and tended by the nurse bees. Now they are starved and
dragged outside the hive, and even stung to death.

The nectar flow of the autumn develops the last brood into

young bees to winter over. The field bees of the summer are ragged and worn and are not replaced in full numbers. Throughout the cold months, the remaining bees congregate inside the hive on the brood chamber. Now indeed they need the honey they have stored. Continuous motion of their wings provides queen and bees with an even temperature inside the cluster. All winter the cluster itself moves like a dark veil over the stored cells of honey, and the cold bees on the outside work themselves down through the cluster and out again. Thus, unlike the lemmings which also respond to food with increase of population and to crowding with mass migration, the bees have an orderly system for reducing population. Lemmings die at random. But the social fabric of the bees is kept intact through the adversity of winter. This system operates regularly every year.

The control system of the bees is programmed by feedback stimuli—too little hive space or too low a honey flow. The bee does not have to "think" about it. The trigger levels for response are probably very precise for each particular variety of bee. But human kinships have more diverse stimuli; where the bee has no choice to make, man has had to decide for many centuries when to move, when to look for more water or food. During these centuries, races of men have endured, while individuals have starved or died in battle. In the human community, as well as in the hive, the female reproducers are the last to starve, the last to be exposed in battles. Larvae of the bee or an embryo of the human may die in adversity, but the female parent survives to try again in better times.

This very protection of the human mother has now become a threat in our control system because she is sheltered from feedback stimuli. It is no accident that girls of sixteen and seventeen yearn for babies; that young mothers want more children and want them sooner than young fathers. For sound biologic reasons the young mother is cheerfully blind to threats which get through to the male.

The human situation differs from the loon, from the lemming and from the bee. It would be helpful if we had an animal like ourselves to study in the wild. But we do not seem to behave like any of the modern anthropoids. The forces which developed modern man failed to develop his anthropoid cousins of long ago into any closely related species. In spite of the great variety of humans, from Eskimos to Kalahari bushmen, we are isolated as a species, able only to stare at ourselves for hopeful clues about our nature, our past and our future.

Human kinships were stable due to a long childhood, which in primitive conditions meant a long sibling relation. The ten or twelve years of close association led to close adult ties; holding cousins together, binding nephew and niece to uncle and aunt, providing a broad-based supervision for the young. Humans seemed to have developed social units from simple kinships of the extended family.

About 10,000 years ago post-glacial improvement in climate opened up new lands to primitive man. We spread with shocking rapidity from the Mediterranean and Afro-Asian centers to all corners of the globe. We began to multiply. We do not know how many people actually crossed over the northern land bridge and down into the Americas, but it does not need to have been a numerous migration. Human populations of 5,000 seem adequate to form distinct peoples. The total Indian population of North America before the white man is guessed to have been less than one million. We do not know what external factors harvested this population, what internal factors prevented them from exploiting their fertility. But in a relatively abundant land they developed patterns of living in which density offered no advantage.

Today, human populations have disordered their own external controls. Most peoples now breed faster than they die off, with a consequent growth of population. At this point in time, no external adversity is rebalancing births with deaths. Until very recently, winter claimed an annual toll of excess deaths from all temperate zone peoples. Pneumonia killed the very old and the very young. TB, childbed fever, infant diarrheas, war and accidents, together with waves of sudden virulence in common disease combined to winnow a hardy species. Over thousands of centuries increase came only slowly. But in the last century the toll of death from every cause except war has dropped dramatically. Sulfa, penicillin, clean water, and more food makes human death come at the end rather than the beginning of life.

Our situation resembles that of the deer herd of Pennsylvania in the 1930's. By then, the original hardwood and white pine forest had been entirely cut over. Lush browse over a large range and a stern campaign to eradicate wolves led to survival of fawns and a rapid increase in numbers of deer. This enlarged population also became sexually out of balance, because only the bucks were legal to shoot in the gunning season.

Dry years in the 1930's brought forest fire, destroying the low brush. Also, many acres were by then maturing into second-growth forest over the heads of the deer. Overbalance of does per buck brought additional crisis. Does normally breed in the fall to fawn in April and May, but for lack of bucks to serve them, many went barren until February and then dropped August fawns. These late fawns were too small by the onset of cold weather to survive the winter. The herds suffered and died. Over thousands of acres of forest a deer-line gave silent evidence of hunger. Every reachable twig and leaf was nipped off even as a hedge.

Spurred by tragedy, we have since found ways to manage these herds. Man has replaced the wolf as predator. Does as well as bucks are harvested annually in a gunning season heavy enough to remove the increase. Wooded areas are again partly in low browse due to rotation of forest cuttings. Deer produce plentifully in balance with browse, and are now an important unfenced domestic livestock.

Humans are like and unlike the deer. Deer could not know

as they died in their winter yards and the fawns were dropped out of season what was happening to them.

But we know.

We know that modern science has removed the external controls, the diseases and hunger which limited human populations over thousands of years. But like the deer herd, we have seemed helpless to take any steps which can restore the balance.

The Logic of Stop at Two

3

IF INDEED we have to achieve a balance between people and resources, if people must live within the green world dependent on oxygen, space, food and water—all of them limited—then our intellectual grasp of this problem is urgent.

No instinct, no invisible external control or stalking predator will rescue us or the world as we have known it. However, in controlling population deliberately, we run against the grain of ancient desires and predilections. Therefore, social and emotional changes, must take place which will lead to fewer births. But first, intelligence, which has led us out of so many savageries in the past must outline the problem.

The first practical step we can take is to state a voluntary population target and discuss it widely. STOP AT TWO permits couples to replace themselves if they can, and yet it does not encourage undue contributions to the next generation. STOP AT TWO does not excuse the couple who is rich or fertile, who *wants* children, who is indifferent to the number arriving, or merely ignorant. It seems just as wrong for the rich to have deliberate ten-child families, as for the poor to have ten children because they are too deprived to prevent it. There is dawning awareness that not only does the rich parent support his large family but he uses an undue proportion of the world's narrowing resources to do so.

Stop at Two is fair to everyone. But the arithmetic of Stop

at Two must become more familiar, a natural part of understanding.

Over the centuries, two parents producing two children would develop a stationary population provided that the survival of children to reproduce in their turn was very high. Before this century survival into adulthood varied from year to year, and for most human populations was by no means dependable enough to permit replacement to take place with only two births.

When 10% of women of reproductive age do not have children either because they are single or infertile, the other 90% provide the next generation. Then the replacement figure per couple for America becomes 2.2 children surviving to reproduce. The fraction allows for replacement of those individuals who do not have children. Because infant mortality in the United States is extremely low, we have come to assume that an average of 2.2 *births* will replace the population. However, where infant mortality is high, more than 2.2 births may be necessary to produce two survivors. Since demographers assume there may be third children even when two are wanted, and since no one has fractions of babies, a voluntary target of Stop at Two reflects closely enough the demographic facts of American replacement.

Even if every family were to stop at two, our population in this century would grow from the level of 200 million reached in 1969 toward 280 million, because of the enlarged breeding population expected from the war babies of twenty years ago. Even if *they* all stop at two, expansion is still inevitable for some decades. Not even the economic establishment which used to rejoice over a new bumper crop of babies is now rejoicing over this squeeze on everything which is in short supply: clean water, clean air, housing, jobs, recreation, education. It is suddenly very clear that increased national prosperity comes from increased goods and services per person, and not from an increase of persons. This is the logic behind Stop at Two.

If every family were to stop at two, differences in generation time would become even more important than at present. Within the United States we not only have differences in racial and religious origins, but, however defined, we have distinct ranges of human quality. Some breed early, some breed late. Until recently, in English and European educated classes, the generation time was roughly thirty-three years for males, while peasants reproduced in a generation time much nearer twenty years. Early students of this difference argued that it would soon submerge the intelligent in a sea of ordinary and less-than-ordinary people. Upward mobility into the ruling classes has not altered the pattern. Families moving upward need more education and a longer start, and quickly take on the delayed marriage pattern which permits it. Upper classes today still have a longer generation time, and are still providing leadership. In any society, under any form of government, the ruling class is not ruling because of its numbers, but because it produces effective leaders.

Sir Francis Galton studied twins and their ability in an effort to sort out the facts of inheritance of intelligence. *Hereditary Genius* is a landmark in the early books on human heredity and Darwinian controversy. Since his day, civil rights unrest has made studies like his deeply unpopular. Yet men are not created equal in a genetic sense and no scientist really pretends that they are. Men are not equal in social value either. Regardless of our desire to think otherwise, some men are not valuable no matter what is done for them, and some men do not want to be valuable. Too much attention to environment has prevented critical study of such problems. Even though environment, and especially the language skills of the family, influence a baby's mental growth and grasp of the world, the greatest attention to environment will not erase inborn difference.

Galton found that identical twins are similar in intelligence but diverge from other brothers and sisters. Furthermore, he documented the prominence attained by members of certain families over several generations. For the welfare of all, perhaps individuals of ability and families of prominent service should reproduce at a faster rate than the rest of us. We do not know. Galton's families do not seem to have been prominent *because* of numerous members, nor did they have to reproduce faster in order to remain prominent. There is no reason to believe a two-child family norm would decrease the percentage of exceptional individuals, nor the prominence of exceptional families. Galton's work has often been represented as genetic snobbery. His pioneering studies may seem curious to us. But we should value his concern for the society he loved. He sincerely approved the kind of "genius" or public ability which he studied. His pages are littered with the names of solicitors, judges, doctors, ministers and university dons. In an amusing document he traces the trend to extinction which the rich heiress brought to her husband's line. An heiress comes from a subfertile line, warns Galton. Otherwise siblings or cousins would have reduced her wealth.

Galton's studies are the first to be deeply concerned by the impact of family size and differential breeding. His blunt desire for native "genius" to hold its own in the British population sounds refreshing to our oversensitized ears. For his studies touch a chord of deep anxiety felt by all kinds of Americans—now that each little ethnic island seems threatened by our population sea. Galton believed, as we would be foolish not to believe, that ability which is not just inborn but which also comes to fruition in public service is a valuable asset to the country. The conditions under which it can be inherited and encouraged to flourish concern everyone. Galton's families emerge from obscurity and sink back again after making their contribution. Properly understood, his work offers no pretext for the rich or the prominent to overbreed.

Opponents of birth control and abortion often use the powerful emotional plea: What wonderful people you are preventing from being born! Suppose it were an Einstein or a Beethoven? In fact, real genius may crop up at any time. Two parents can provide so many thousands of genetic combinations that not even in the largest family can the best one have more than a rare chance of being born. Our desire for genius to be born and somehow set right all that is wrong with our world does not bear on the question of how many of us ought to live on the earth at any one time.

We know the death rates from cancer and suicide and car accidents in America, but we can hardly conclude that we are preventing these disasters in proportion by preventing so many thousands of births. Nor are we preventing genius. About the fate of a child who never was born, we can make no valid assertions.

We might have cause to worry about Stop at Two if all or even a majority of gifted individuals were third or higher in birth order. There are more first and second children in any country than there are subsequent children, of course. As higher birth orders decrease in the trend to small families, ability should still occur at the same rate as before if birth order is not involved. However, if high birth order is a factor producing ability, ability should concentrate in those relatively few large families. Aside from practical problems in defining ability and measuring its occurrence, computers have made it much easier for us to study questions of this kind.

There is not the least evidence at the present time that the two-child family will reduce the apparently random incidence of genius. There is not the least evidence that ability is restricted to the rich or the educated. But there is evidence we ought to face that certain families excel others in services rendered to society. Often over long periods of time, societies have depended on such families. Today the right to be different, the right to excel has received little of our attention. We need to know what spurs on individuals, and to study the family dynamics which support the efforts of outstanding sons and daughters. Encouragement of hereditary genius is a task for human ecology.

Genetics and human selection, hybrid vigor and breeding isolation operate in human populations as they do in those of birds and other animals. Any breeding program will have genetic impact, and be selective of the next generation. Stop at Two is proposed instead of the natalist program which is now in rampant mid-career.

Our present program has not been studied; no authorities recommend it. We have been flung into it by the headlong acceleration of disease control, of death control, of suddenly improved nutrition. Now, suddenly recognizing the disaster and collecting ourselves, we have no time to sit and study the situation. We are in danger of being studied to death. It is safe and fashionable to finance studies rather than action. Ironically, in the crisis in population, political and religious leaders encourage "studies" as delaying tactics, while the scientists cry for action. But one does not study a disaster until afterward. One gets rescued first.

What we need is a breathing spell. We need to halt in our tracks. But tremendous forces are needed to brake a car traveling at seventy miles an hour. We are rushing into a doubling-time for the now living population which is much faster than seventy years. Coming to a halt will take huge pressure. However the gloomy who do not believe population growth can be stopped reckon without the very population producing it. If, because the need is clear, couples *want* one or two children, the task will be done. It will not depend on methods nor wait for study. If two children suddenly becomes the pattern required for surviving, the species has had an overwhelming instinct for that. Men and women can be trusted to respond. We are not sure of the shape or the size of the danger. But our social and scientific lookouts have given warning.

For crows in a corn field or deer sampling new grain, it is the lookout who gives the signal for emergency. In modern human populations, contrary to crows, we dispute signals from the lookouts, and argue and ask for proof. But crows rising in a flock, or deer bounding away one after another obey danger signals first, and reconnoiter afterward.

The Arithmetic of Stop at Two

4

ARITHMETIC HAS no color. Logic has no skin. Everyone is having too many babies.

But if everyone is having too many children, what can be done to understand the logic and arithmetic? We ought to be learning it in school and with our income-tax forms and our social security chits—because our schools and our income and our social security depend upon understanding the logic and arithmetic of population growth!

A stable population depends upon the balance of births with deaths on the one hand, and a balance of the living with their resources on the other. The total size of a population depends upon the age at which death intervenes.

Longer life means stretching out the cycle of calcium and iron and rarer ions so that more of them are locked up in living bodies at any one time. Demands for space and air and fuel are also increased by a long-lived population. Such a shift from early to late death occurred in many countries with the advent of western science and medicine after World War II.

But such a picture oversimplifies because nothing is static about a population to which such dramatic change occurs. Twenty years after the change to late death, we suddenly have an enlargement of the reproducing population. Babies which formerly would have died have survived to produce children. Parents Jane and John replaced themselves with Jane and John, Jr. But they did more than that. Now their third and fourth children also live to have children. Parents John and Jane have doubled themselves. In conditions of early death, of high infant mortality, only John and Jane, Jr. might have survived. But with later death the extra siblings make an expanded base, from which population expands again.

The monolith can occur only where late death is the rule and where births do not exceed the replacement number for that particular population. Almost no growth occurs here. A shape of this kind means births and deaths are balanced, with high survival into late years and relatively low rates of reproduction. Here the number of people in productive ages compares well both with young children and aged dependents. Sweden's stable population has not avoided labor shortages, housing shortages or strange internal migrations. But it does seem to have avoided the absolute increase of misery evident in other population profiles.

What we find more commonly in the world today is a series of population jumps, like that which occurred in 1946 in America. In 1967, four million instead of three million young people turned twenty-one and the four million rate will continue for many years. The expected steep rise in total numbers in the United States is due not only to increased births and survival to breeding age, but to the increase expected from this increase. If those extra sons and daughters born in 1946 and years following also raise extra sons and daughters to reproducing age, stability in the United States is far away. Growth will continue.

No conflict between generations has ever been so important. The adults who were the last explosive agents in a long sequence of population increase stand on one side. The young reproducer stands on the other. Rejection of war, of poverty, of spoiled environment may be essential to the human future. But rejection of births is the most critical shift of all. The human creature will have to look elsewhere than to the womb for guarantees of human value.

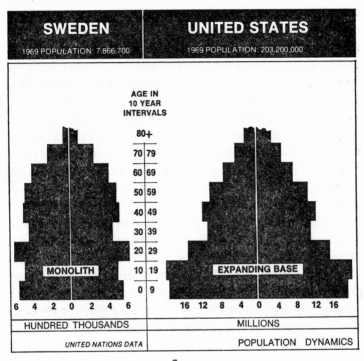

fig. 1

In addition to the problem of increase on the increase, we have the impact of age at first birth. In many Asian countries, a woman's age at first birth was once as low as fourteen. For several decades the age at first birth has been rising in these countries, while it has been falling in western societies, including our own. We have good evidence that the improved nutrition of the past thirty years or more in America is having its effect. Both girls and boys are coming to sexual maturity a year and a half earlier than they did in the last century. Sexual as well as social conditions in the west are favoring earlier marriage and earlier childbearing. This has had large effects on population in the past. Early childbearing usually means larger completed families and certainly means shorter time between generations. If we look just at generation time, we can recognize several important facts.

If a first male has his first child at thirty-three, his father will be sixty-six and his grandfather ninety-nine. If a first male has his first child at twenty, his father will be forty and his grandfather sixty. It is possible that he will have living great-grandparents of eighty. Requirements for food, money, jobs, housing, nutrients in scarce supply are quite different for these two families. A farm or business can pass from a father of sixty-six to a son of thirty-three; but in the second family, with possibly a parent still alive at eighty, the sixty-year-old man still has himself and his wife to think of, and the son of forty is far from ready to displace himself from the family farm or business enterprise to make way for *his* son. Such a pattern is more suited to an urban family with little to pass on or divide up, and is common among families on wages or welfare.

If we take five steps of a stairway for our family of twenty years generation time, and three steps of a stair for the family with thirty-three years, and now we add to each appropriate step a different number of children, we can see how these two factors will compound a differential growth rate. This differential is the source of hatred and fear between stable groups and flagrantly outbreeding ones, between management and labor, the landowner and the worker. Earlier sexual maturity places strain upon a society marrying late. The trend toward financing married students may cut into the delay of the highly educated, but all over the world the lower birth rate and longer generation time of educated and professional families is a fact of our technical century.

Part of the peculiar arithmetic of human populations lies in these ideas. The more impoverished the people, the more children they have and the quicker the generation time. This was formerly compensated for by high infant deaths. But everywhere in the world infant mortality has been falling. It has fallen fastest since World War II in just those countries where it provided the most severe check on population. India, Morocco, and Egypt are suffering the most intense growth of all, and among the poorest sections of their people. As a consequence, the generation of young people coming to breeding age all over the world presents an incredible increase over their parents' generation. In the children they may expect to have in the next few years, they will be laying up a powder train with a twenty-year fuse. What will be the increase on this increase twenty years from now?

Such a question is often answered in terms of rates—birth rates, growth rates, fertility rates. The time unit is a year, and the base depends upon accurate census figures for total population, births, deaths and the number of women in the reproductive ages. The simplest comparison, often made in the press, is that of one country's birth rate with that of another. Birth rate is an expression of the number of births per thousand of the total population that year. We must know total population and total births for these countries, or we cannot arrive at a birth rate. For many countries such figures are inaccurate. One of the important works of the U. N. has been to foster and standardize census-taking in member countries.

Birth rate, while seeming the simplest measure, is deceptive.

We can have two countries with the same birth rate, and yet the numbers of babies born in them can be very different. A birth rate of eighteen in a small country means much less demand on world resources than a birth rate of eighteen in a large country like the United States, because total growth of population is a function of the number of thousands involved. In 1933 the United States had a birth rate of eighteen per thousand. But it involved many fewer total births than it did in 1970—2¼ versus 3½ million.

Annual growth rate gives a more revealing comparison between countries. Here death rate is subtracted from birth rate and reduced to per cent. For the United States,

$$18/1000 - 9/1000 = 9/1000 \text{ or } 0.9\%.$$

This was our estimated rate in 1968. Even more useful is a ten-year moving average because the 22/1000 birth rate of 1963 became 17/1000 in 1969, and may either be 22/1000 again by 1973 or may continue to drop.

A 1% growth rate would mean doubling in one hundred years, except for the increase every year which must be figured in. Compounding this increase pulls the doubling-time down. A useful rule of thumb is to remember that a 1% growth rate per year means doubling in seventy years. Doubling the rate of growth halves the doubling-time. Other rates can be figured from this. A 2% rate doubles in thirty-five years; 4% doubles in eighteen years.

A growth rate for the United States of 0.9% per annum does not sound very alarming. We are growing at less than 1% a year. A nation that does not object to a 15% charge on installment plans is hard to shock with a figure 0.9%. But let us turn it into people.

For every mouth to feed now, and car to drive, there would be another beside it in eighty years. This is just long enough to excuse us, and stick the next generation. It will not be at *our* elbow that this living shadow stands, waiting for one-half of our share.

During the last century, even with continually expanding resources, we have just managed to stay ahead of increase in our population in this country. But other countries, settled for thousands of years without our economic base and skilled workers, have not been able to keep pace with the rise of their population. We too, are at last facing the fact that a country rich with two hundred million has stark pockets of poverty. With three hundred million seriously predicted for us in the near future we, like the rest of the world, may be facing the logic and arithmetic of too many people.

Why is it so difficult to recognize our disaster and deal with it soon enough? Growth rates are like interest at the bank. Increase on the increase is paid in money and this interest goes back in, to increase again. But money at the bank pays interest right along. What lulls us into false security is that babies do not produce their increase for some twenty years (or whatever the average age at first birth). The final impact of the roughly 3.5 million babies born this year will not be felt for forty years when they will have completed their families. When a birth rate falls but total births are on the rise, it is easy to neglect this explosive time factor. We are about to reap the harvest of the post-war baby boom begun in the late forties. For every existing thousand, the number of young couples entering breeding age is rising. Birth rate will bound back up again in a few years when these young couples are in full swing.

The total size of our population in the next century depends upon these young couples, and on what steps they take to limit their families. For adults of today it is already too late to provide the remedy. The situation is out of their hands. The most drastic curtailment of births by couples over twenty-five will not be significant unless couples under twenty-five will stop at two. Stop at Two would barely hold the line at three hundred million. Yet our past attitudes toward national reproduction give us little encouragement to think that even this can be done.

In the United States we breed at the rate of three and one-half million per year. The total casualties of the Vietnam War come far below one million. We cannot conceive of a sufficient military loss of young lives to rebalance our population in the next century. Such loss by disease and starvation seems equally unthinkable. Only mass failure to breed can readjust massive overbreeding in any humane way. But mass refusal to breed is not easily brought about, especially since it is nobody's problem, nobody's objective.

How Dense Can We Be?

5

WHENEVER WE PROPOSE to limit births or sanction merciful death, protests arise because of the sanctity of human life. In the west particularly, earlier generations did indeed take Christian vows to revere life, to preserve it, in their military orders, in medicine, church and law. It never occurred to them and it had never occurred in nature that sheer human survival could become the worst of all dangers. Fortunately men have never had to live anywhere near the maximum possible density.

We need to ask ourselves not how densely we could live, how many we could feed, but what is good about such density? Who wants to breed or feed or shelter so many people? To protect the sanctity of human life is not to defend its unlimited quantity.

If we are not condemned to an irreversible crescendo of human numbers, it might be worthwhile to explore where our optimum density may be.

The west is just now admitting that technology and pollution increase together, spurred on by the demands of ever more consumers. As technology removes new material from the earth, and adds pollution back into it, it also leaves behind an ever narrower margin of unspoiled resources. For these reasons of dwindling resource and rising pollution, many people consider our optimum density already well behind us.

After millennia in which we have increased and covered the globe to its furthest and most forbidding corners, we have reached the point of basic change that catches up to all expanding species. Species come to equilibrium or to wild fluctuation. Humans also will have to settle for stable numbers, otherwise the diseases of violence and disorder will ravage our social fabric. The very systems which make density possible will break down, because above a critical density we cannot help ourselves. We are beginning to share a worldwide feeling that human populations will be happier if they persist for future centuries in relatively stable numbers.

Riots and disorders are occurring not only in America but worldwide. Persuasive political or economic reasons are given for them. They are blamed on racism, hunger, lack of opportunity, lack of powers. But it is disturbing to wonder if the common denominator is not in fact a subrational reaction to one single factor—crowding.

Neither concessions from government nor repressive controls will quell civil unrest. In fact, these measures will prove costly and misleading if the major cause of unrest is density. No solution or concession yet proposed involves direct reduction of density.

The intellectual young feel the pressures of crowding more than adults. Pressure to compete conflicts with intense pressure to conform in a dense society. Behavior which was tolerable in spaced-out patterns—wild driving on empty roads, a car or two full of lovers, a beach party singing far into the night—have become mob races, beach orgies, chanting sit-ins and love-ins. Part of what we know as student protest is the boiling-over of normal needs of young people, acting in abnormal masses. Trying to apply old rules to these events merely leads to further protest.

The young know with a kind of bitterness that they might take time to enjoy their children more than they were enjoyed themselves. But on top of many other ecologic difficulties they know they must deny themselves the refuge of having children. While opinion shifts the callous will continue to bring children into the world regardless, but the concerned will limit this pleasure. As new patterns move up from school to college young couples will respond and stop at two, while older couples go right on. For a short time, such inequities cannot be avoided.

To be *for* life we must often appear to be against it. To develop truly equal opportunities we must seem to be against equality and for excellence. We must resist the tendency of crowded societies to mass-produce non-people. Instead, we want them taught, by loving parents and other kin, by a school tailored to the child and his language, to the mother and her culture. Most of all, children need to grow by themselves in their own way, in their own minimum of space and freedom. The great enterprise of stuffing empty minds with useless facts has broken down. Does anyone believe that children can be allowed their childhood or loved with a relaxing gaiety? We have to believe it. Nothing less is enough.

Political programs tailored to production and moon races go goose-stepping past with ears deaf to the cry for more lovely creatures in a more joyful world. No one in America expects to die of famine. But many Americans never expect to be joyful. As one young school boy bitterly put it, most adults would not know how to be happy even if they *were* happy. This is nowhere near enough dream for the American dream.

In the drive to small families, every value of the large family is certain to be sacrificed. The large family is as out of date, as unsuited to the contest, as the dinosaur. The merits claimed for it will look bizarre to subsequent populations. It is hard for the momentarily ruling age groups to have all their values— money, education, manners, race, and the large family—challenged at once by the march of events. It is hardest of all to be taught hard facts by the young.

Social unrest, however, might finally shift from struggles over jobs, money and political power to resentful overbreeding in those segments of the world's people in which it would be the cruelest disaster. Use of fertility as a weapon is not new, but in modern terms it is the grimmest menace that could arise. If a ruthless population exploded its share of the gene pool, stable and basically responsible populations would react to the threat. It is appalling to consider the situation the world would face if competing populations were triggered into a race. What advantages could be gained, and by whom? What could be termed "success"?

In modern evolutionary theory, the "success" of a population is termed its "fitness". By definition, biologic fitness is measured in terms of the number of offspring surviving to reproduce.

If two of A's ten children survive to reproduce, and three out of B's three do so, B is more fit than A. More of B's genes will show up in the gene pool of the next generation.

A's two survivors now have ten each, just as their parents had ten. Suddenly modern medicine permits eight out of each ten to survive and reproduce. Meanwhile B's three children each have three, all of whom grow up to reproduce. Now the situation is dramatically reversed. In the first generation, B was more fit with fewer children born. In the second generation, A's children are more fit with more children born. So fitness is distinct from being fertile or prolific. Those raising the most young to maturity are not necessarily producing the most.

If we pursue the "success" story of A and B a little further, we find them as grandparents of sixteen and nine children born into the world of modern disease control. A had raised two children and was less fit than B who raised three. But in one generation, A became more "fit" with sixteen grandchildren than B with nine.

In today's cities, the outcome is even more uncertain. The nine born to B's three children stand a better chance of being educated and fed than the sixteen born to A's two children. It makes a difference whether nine mouths are being fed by three fathers at work or sixteen mouths by two fathers. Only in a country or a family rich enough to ignore the labor per child fed, can the sixteen children expect as much out of life as the nine, or give as much to it. It makes a great difference whether our reverence for human life concerns its quality or only its quantity. This colors the meaning we will give to success.

In even worse circumstances, the presence of the sixteen plus nine threatens all the children together with the cumulative effects of crowding, malnutrition and eventual hunger. Old patterns of large families, ideals of fertility and many pregnancies are thus *not* required in breeding success. True success in times of crowding, in bad times, may mean having only one!

A dramatic shift of fitness is usually caused not by the behavior of the species undergoing change, but by a change in external conditions. Change of human population over the last decades has not been brought about by change in reproductive behavior, but by changes in controlling disease. Population explosions occur in species which do not compensate quickly for such changes. But "quickly" is a relative word. It will be wonderful and extraordinary if human populations can accommodate to disease control in the course of even three generations. But meanwhile the price paid by the poorer members of these three generations seems intolerable. If reason can control births, it seems utterly unreasonable not to. No other relief would help so many so quickly. Scientists and philosophers lose their "cool" when exposed to the conditions under which millions of children must live today. Their urge to "do something" is intense. Here again relations are upside down. The politicians and theologians recommend caution and delay. Science, so methodical, urges action.

Fitness defined merely as breeding success means that the most fit species can quickly create an impasse for itself by overbreeding. New investigations in ecology and ethology are altering our acceptance of such a simple definition of biological success. Any long-term survival of a species as victor in competition for food or territory has involved adaptation of breeding behavior. Human conflicts, for example, have not been decided on the basis of numbers only, but rather of persistence. Small nations have defended themselves famously against a more numerous invader. We have only just begun to reexamine the notion of territory. No animal findings are yet brought down convincingly to human terms. But we know that some of the most durable forms of life are never numerous. Very stable populations can also be quite sparse as we have seen in the case of the loons.

It is not necessarily the rare animals who vanish. Long before humans came to kill off herds of buffalo and vast flocks of passenger pigeons, great waves of animal populations surged over the earth and vanished. We have failed to discover why the dinosaurs died off at a time when their dominance seems to have been at its height. Climate change which somehow permitted the rise of descendant primates seems to have permitted other survivals too. Snakes and lizards persist. The modern climate has brought brilliance, diversity, and the puzzle of migration to birds, descendants of a dinosaur contemporary. Yet today, only in the Galapagos do the rock-swarming iguanas even faintly suggest that monster domination of the past. Was it sheer numbers which denied them viable descendants? Perhaps they were like the pure stand of alfalfa, or white pine, or cotton wiped out too easily because of their density.

We also could be cut down too easily by the wildfire of plague or influenza, whereas the old, spaced-out landed patterns of human life allowed virulence to exhaust itself and variety to develop. Only in the air age have all the ailments of the world threatened all its people. Only in the age of modern sanitation and control of disease have people themselves become an epidemic which threatens disaster. We must come to accept a fluctuation of peoples within narrow limits as normal, tolerable and self-limiting. It has occurred throughout a long human history, but we must now control fertility outbreaks and avoid competitive breeding.

Like an embroidered silk, the colors of birds flash through the green forest. Like an ancient tapestry, the human race has paraded its colors and costumes and brilliant folkways across the variable earth. Species of birds have vanished, civilizations have fallen into ruin, but no bird has displaced all the others, no human race has swept the earth. Everywhere the pattern, the variety, above all the balance remain. Today, to protect the pattern and variety, to keep the precarious and ever-shifting balance, most human parents will need to stop at two.

We are not the only species to retreat from over-fertility and to accept limits on reproduction. Seabirds have developed complex delaying tactics, especially the kittiwakes who nest in offshore rookeries where space is at a premium. A nesting territory is essential because the chick must be secure during the long fishing flights of the adults away from the rook. In the contest for space even second- and third-year males are denied a territory. But to be without a territory is to be without a mate. Late to breed, often raising only one chick a year, these birds express an aggressive sex drive, but the need to protect the young produced is even stronger.

In this respect, the European titmouse is especially interesting. One strain lays one egg a year and raises one chick. The other strain lays two or three eggs, but often fails to raise any because feeding three mouths on freshly captured insects requires too much from the parents. The energy-budget of the young demands constant protein; the energy-budget of the parent must cope with hunting and feeding flights lasting from daybreak to dusk. Catching-time and flight distance vary with insect supply from year to year. Failure to give any one chick enough food ends in weakness and death for all. In bad years, the three-egg titmice are like ourselves. Instead of choosing one chick and letting the others die, they try to raise them all. Three-egg titmice survive as a small population because every few years, often enough to even the balance, a year comes along when insect life is extraordinarily abundant and all the titmice raise out the maximum number of chicks from eggs hatched.

Careful experiments proved that for these titmice, egg number is an inherited trait. These two genetic types combine to stabilize the overall population of the species against fluctuating conditions. Here the problem to be solved in nature was not how to produce more eggs, but how to conserve hatched chicks in years of adversity. The solution concentrates energy on limited production. These active interesting dooryard birds offer a noted example of what is called stable polymorphism. Both kinds of titmice are expected to be around a long time in fairly dependable numbers. Together they increase the survival rates of titmice.

A Catholic pope or a militant black leader who expects overbreeding to provide his power base is less sensitive to the needs of his young, or to conditions in their world, than pelagic birds or the little titmouse. And people are less fortunate than flocks of birds, for bird controls are still instinctive, inherited—beyond the reach of leaders to lead astray.

The Twice-minded

6

MANY OF THE PEOPLE most interested in discussing population are twice-minded about it. Population is growing too fast for housing, food, jobs, pollution control, and so on. These people readily admit this and then say with another part of their minds, "So we will grow more food, develop new jobs, build houses faster." They do not realize that population is a problem in itself requiring single-minded population solutions. Housing problems can be solved by housing, job problems by jobs, food problems by food. But none of these by themselves nor all together, will solve population problems.

For any population, there is an absolute upper limit, and an absolute lower limit. There are optimum levels, and conditions of density above and below optimum. These vary with the intrinsic energy-relations between people: the point where cooperation falls off and competition rises to an unhealthy level. The values which are threatened by population above a certain density are not merely related to higher material living standards. They are related to kinds of living. But we have no simple, well-understood names for these values. Because we have had to hunt, eat, burn, chop, build, our languages for these activities are well developed. We understand each other when we talk food and shelter and money. But we have only just come to the point where density bothers us, where the irritations of noise, voice, presence have penetrated our collective awareness. We are irresponsible in new ways, angry in new ways which are hard for us to understand. Our language is not well developed for explaining why we are irritated. It is still in the textbooks and laboratories, and not yet coined on the street.

The generation gap is partly a function of density. The young no longer have a place to move into because the old are not yet ready to move out. But the gap is of language too. Lack of communication is noticed by everyone, as though it were somebody's fault. Common language, shared experience can develop over time, and under pressure of consensus. In the greatly specialized densities of urban living, common experience and consensus on meaning is harder to come by. We are all somewhat like a four-year-old who is convinced that tears and shouting, smashing and smearing will somehow make up for the fact that others lack understanding of his private language. He has not yet developed enough notion of "others" to use their public language. We seem to be shouting at each other in private languages about the unfamiliar pressures of a too-crowded world.

Many unpleasant feelings: anxiety, loneliness, a sense of uselessness, of not belonging have become more common, more unpleasant. But the direct relation between these feelings and the density experience of modern man has not been well investigated. Striking experiments by John Calhoun (1962) have demonstrated it in rats. Calhoun's experimental series provides a genuine analogy to our population experience: a limited space, an unlimited food supply, and a small initial population. Given enough food, the animals breed up to and beyond the optimum density. They continue to breed while all normal patterns of social relations break down. Young are deserted, males are sterile, adults die of stress. Leaving much of the cage empty they crowd into a central mass.

Rat-man and rat behavior is a fact of our scene, and these experiments in themselves tell us less perhaps than do the aversion and denial reactions they arouse in the general public. No one likes to think about rat-man but we must, for sincere humans believe that we can and should develop unlimited food supplies, and that this will solve our problems. The pope in his speech on population said just this: because governments have not yet done enough to supply their peoples, they must not limit peoples.

We know that we are not going to increase food supplies as fast as we increase ourselves. The World Congress of Botanists said this most clearly in 1969. If we were to increase food by the amount necessary to avert the famines predicted for the seventies world reaction would be one of intense relief. We would look upon the varieties of hybrid Mexican wheat which might make this possible as lifesaving, wonderful. But solving a specific shortage of food with a specific increase in grain harvest is the single-minded solving of a food problem. It is not the solving of a population problem. It will not lead to optimum density. People will still have to occupy houses, find work, drink water, and produce waste. They still have to live near each other in densities fixed by the nature of land-ownership and farm-village relations. Too many people is too many whether they are hungry or not. Where human life is cheap, and fate is all-powerful, bias toward life is less acute. In such countries reduction in population is more easily recognized as a desirable goal in itself, just as producing more food is a desirable goal.

We are angry and have no proper language for our new experiences. Also it seems as though there were a special fixity in human attitudes. The four-year-old who cannot figure out what another is telling him becomes extremely intense. He repeats his efforts and concentrates on shouting out a single word or idea as the clue. Perhaps we are as new as four-year-olds in dealing with such massive human numbers; perhaps to realize how difficult we are, we need to observe ourselves from another perspective.

The Chalicodoma of the walls is a handsome bee of the Camargue, the delta of the Rhone Valley near Marseilles. She builds a little mud pot for her eggs, carrying the clay mouthful by mouthful and smoothing it inside and out. When the masonry is finished, she becomes a supplier of honey and not of houses.

A tiny hole pierced in the underside of the mud while she is building causes her to fly off and mend it immediately with fresh clay. But if she has already started to fill the nest with honey, so that the honey flows out when it is pierced, the bee will carry honey to the jar for some time without finding the hole. Then she finds it. She inspects it carefully, seems excited and flies off quickly, to return with more honey!

This resembles the behavior of human population specialists. They propose solutions and improve crops and housing enormously. But people are still crowded and still hungry. In consternation the experts rush around in consultation and go off to develop new programs of ?—more food and more housing! Their progress, their vital energies are draining away through the flaw of too-rapid population increase. They never suspect they are like the Chalicodoma of the walls. The honey flows unplugged from the nest of the bee. Her efforts are useless. Her instincts are too inflexible to permit her to go back and repair the hole. We, too, seem to have become inflexible experts. When our remedies fail to work, we, too, are excited and anxious, and rush around with new efforts to produce more of everything except a new solution. Like the bee we cannot recognize that our answers are no answers at all to the real problem. We are twice-minded, staring population problems in the face, and producing everything except a population remedy.

Permissive liberality defeats its own purpose, for we cannot have unlimited people and limited resources! We could devise suitable experiments and expect significant, if not final, answers to the question of how many people we ought to have. But family planning experts are like the cancer patient who fears diagnosis and surgery. We are afraid to discover that we have already passed the optimum density for humans even in

America, and cannot bear the thought of the remedy. We have no option except to produce fewer children, yet even people who sincerely accept the evidence of crowding are not able to make this single-minded decision. As Americans, we hate to admit there may be no options for us since we are especially critical of other governments whose citizens have none. We like to imagine that choice is a vital part of our social system.

Yet day after day we are moving toward less and less choice because we are twice-minded. We are boxing ourselves into ugliness, deficits, unemployment and deteriorating education in the name of freedom to breed as we please. Millions of citizens are unable to understand what is happening to them. Others who are beginning to understand feel trapped in the grip of an unresponsive bureaucracy. It is difficult to pursue even one thought to its faraway conclusion, without being distracted many times on the way. It is difficult to pin responsibility on any official for anything he has done or refuses to do. Seeing both sides can become a national weakness as well as a political skill. As a nation, we can rarely scrape ourselves up over the energy-top to the high level of performance that results from being single-minded.

There are a few people who are single-minded, whose thought follows and hounds an idea, who gnaw it like a bone, who circle back to it again and again. They are not afraid to annoy people with their vision of being right. The imaginative Hindu, Sripati Chandrasekhar, is one demographer who is not twice-minded. As Minister of Family Planning for India he brought a restless consuming energy to every kind of project, pouring a beautiful stream of rhetoric on the opposition. In America, Robert McNamara has been equally lucid and outspoken. But he does not speak from a strong domestic program to reduce American population. All his efforts are thus suspected abroad and found puzzling at home. Only in science and medicine do Americans reward such single-mindedness. In science the task is to uncover the facts, to follow their implications and to be single-minded in pursuing them, no matter what they mean. The scientist brings his experiments, results, and conclusions into a coherent whole which can be tested and found false, or confirmed and put to use. Habitually scientists accept rather quietly the next obvious steps, no matter how difficult or unpleasant.

This is why only the scientific community at present is speaking out on population control. Loyal to the evidence, they are automatically reporting the danger. Politicians can be twice-minded, considering voter reactions instead of the facts. Economists can be twice-minded thinking of productivity, and agriculturists can be twice-minded thinking about more food. The military can be twice-minded thinking about arms races and manpower problems. But the scientist has little to distract him from his projections.

An animal crowding his range becomes dangerous, disoriented and unpredictable and the range can only deteriorate under pressure. The single-minded conclusion is to cut back the crowding—and we would have done so radically for any other species but our own. What prevents us are unexplored fears. If we cut back our population, must a depression follow? Must there be all kinds of social evils or unhappiness which we can not predict but which we dread? Evidence points the other way. The population problem lends itself to pleasing solutions, while not solving it will be very unpleasant indeed!

It is difficult for Americans to be single-minded about any enterprise. In our brief history, we have been twice-minded about many issues, seeing both sides at once, valuing both sides at once, seeking not compromise, but opposite policies at the same time, with an effort that is laudable, even if confusing. We are as proud of these efforts as though they were consistent.

We want the rich to make us all richer, and the poor to have more; we want the farmer to get high prices and the housewife to pay low ones. We want more police protection and less police brutality; as though all this were compatible and might happen. All of the best qualities of America surface in the inconsistent, pluralistic, floundering and yet productive pattern of American life. It would not be an improvement to be coherent, compromising, consistent and regular. It would be a backward step toward the rigid kind of tribal society human beings have been trying to escape from all of their recorded and unrecorded history. Into every constitution in the United States is written discontinuity as the price of freedom. We are twice-minded about even the most prominent among us, if they threaten to stay in power too long. We give them short terms and require campaigns, and can always—so we believe—unseat them at last. We believe that among the welter of options, we can choose what we want and that it will turn out to be good for us. Even though in fact American life is tightly programmed, with twelve years of schooling, the draft, marriage, children, we do not admit it easily; we do not admire it; we make an effort to exempt ourselves and our friends from the universal dilemma. No wonder our politicians are attempting to dodge population control!

Not everyone loves children nor approves of large families. Although our twice-minded society assumes we do, the facts are quite otherwise. Children are often unhappy tools in their parents' social striving, and blocks to friendship. In the small, crowded house children divide rather than unite their parents. They impede the development of personal talent or commercial projects, even in homes aware of their needs. Children are the cruelest weapon in marital fighting and mere pawns in the welfare system. Even if we can reconcile all this with love for children, one fact will not reconcile. A common cause of infant death in U.S. cities is child abuse—not pneumonia, not dysentery, but the battered child. Only the twice-minded could argue that these children have a right to be born. In our society the unwanted child is *unwanted enough* to cause infant death and maternal suicide. Under conditions of crowding, this is how civilized we can become.

In America, thousands of deprived young girls go straight

from childhood to pregnancy, marriage and drudgery without any intervening personal development. In a society which expected more room and fewer people, there would be no need for this kind of deprivation. Delay of first birth until the mother is in her twenties is one population control upon which everyone certainly ought to agree.

Throughout the sixties students knew that their parents had very nice social myths which made living tolerable. Vietnam, poverty and pollution exposed the myths. Students eager for change indicted the system and also chided their parents for succeeding in it. Keynesian economics, planned obsolescence —tax and tax—spend and spend—buy and buy produced a conspicuous prosperity, a plethora of goods and credit cards. Sudden cries of *planned waste, pollution, exploitation, rape of the biosphere* bounce solidly off the selfishness of millions who have been able to "get theirs" for the first time. No back-to-the-bicycle ecology is going to dent their entrenched comfort. Even if terrible, even if deadly, the status quo will last their lifetime! With minor variations the sons of Wall Street and the sons of organized labor hear the very same refrain!

When they were young, the "older" generation believed in World War II, even to the bomb on Hiroshima. They feared communism and financed the UN. To the rash of draftcard burners they replied by waving the flag, not believing their own children could be expressing a new patriotism, a new loyalty. Yet these new patriots, their children, find it terrible for adults to decry civil violence while voting enormous budgets for weapons. Staring at each other across the generation gap, clogged by the same institutions, snowed under by paperwork, defeated by protocol, neither young nor old take stock of their own behavior. Yet "doing your own thing" and succeeding in business are kindred validations of an individual against this mass. Both, in their own stupid ways, are trying to hold onto sharp personal identities against the faceless sea of more people. No wonder Americans are twice-minded, being and begetting the trouble and not believing in it!

Today the luxurious overproduction of children has made them an unmarketable commodity; they lack a sense of being drawn forward into the needs of society. Nothing is changed if they "cop out" as hippies or refuse to use their abilities. Their world has not made them feel either a sense of need or duty. Rather than moving smoothly into the patterns of an adult community that wants them, they are shunted into more education, into the draft or into idleness. While their numbers increase from below, there is no steady withdrawal from above. It is to be hoped they will not pass on this iniquity to *their* children, but will stop at two, or one, or none and set the system in reverse. In *one* generation a single-minded desire for population control would reshape their America.

Instead, the twice-minded policy of the nation looks at the population curve and the census figures. On the basis of extending those curves, as though they were inevitable, we are told how we shall live in ever-more fantastic, unreal, inhuman glass walls and concentrated boxes, and how few will ever live as we do now, with any green world around us, any thick forest or moist grass between us. Nothing at all is said about the green lung which is unique among the planets, perhaps unique among all the stars, and doomed in the long timescale of stars, but need not be doomed by us, by our crazy overbreeding and cutting down and burning up.

Who would slice up their lungs to make houses? Yet we are slicing up the green lung to make plywood, to string phone lines, to build highways and cement cities. No one knows how much of it we need for breathing. We are not likely to know until we have gone too far and find ourselves too numerous in a world that breathes no longer. We are twice-minded. We may understand too late.

Ecology

7

ECOLOGY IS a new set of studies which developed out of the oldest of biological inquiry: natural history and the nature of man. Modern ecology includes the distinctive anatomy and physiology of animals, and their basic behavior in laboratory conditions. But it includes more than this. New attention is being given to animals in their natural habitat; to their food habits, patterns of sleeping and waking, hunting and mating which bear upon other animals and the total community. Some of the most fascinating of modern biologic literature falls into this area of study. Still other ecologists concentrate upon animal numbers; changes in numbers, and patterns of animal distribution.

Advanced techniques of sampling and statistical analysis have led to various models of population change. Many factors affect an animal population: in-and-out migration, disease, predation, sudden heat spells, freezing, drought and flood. Some species seem to fluctuate in regular cycles within rather wide limits; others appear extremely stable over long periods. As usual in statistical studies conflict often ensues between the mathematical lab and the census takers in the field as to the meaning of events. Last of all, community ecologists are inclined to draw on all these disciplines but to add something of their own. Food chains and energy-budgets are followed throughout a meadow, forest edge, or city fishpond. What happens on the exposed side of a bare rock and on the plant-shaded base of it can be strikingly different. Geology, climate, under-and-over-population, all affect the community. Such studies are important for human survival. All of them are even more important for something else, for I believe they hold the clue to retaining in the world the possibility of human joy.

Survival without enjoyment is survival without worship, without love, without hope. Such survival is not talking about human beings but about some sort of truncated descendant of ourselves who may truly live in boxes of cement, eat algae, reproduce by test tube and use plastic pumps for hearts, but who will have lost the great and delightful primitiveness of man. Man as we know him is full of possibility. Man as he is proposing to become will be selecting a one-way ticket to extinction, becoming a population of conformity rushing to a uniform disaster. Separate disasters, separate fates and futures are far more interesting. Also, they are more in keeping with the intense urge toward diversity of form and function which has been expressed by the rise and spread of plants and animals century after century across the surface of the earth.

Diversity provides a wider net to catch and use the energy of sunlight. We are aware today of the fragile ferns, the tough banyan, tropical palm and arctic lichen. We have seen the fragile almost-water bells of jellyfish, the scintillant comb jelly, the delicate brittle stars. We even know that species of the transparent arrow worms, sagitta, mark off one northern ocean current from another. We have only to turn on any TV program of skin diving or safari to be bombarded with the beauty and diversity of form in which living energy can be captured and expressed. We do not realize that we ourselves are one of the more extreme expressions of diversity. Races of men have adapted to extremes of heat and cold, desert and forest, water and mountain. They developed, perfected and abandoned whole cultures and languages. In the effort to live in even larger units, to act as nations or supranations, we sometimes forget to value these diversities.

Perhaps we have no real options. Perhaps we are not able to select for variety and freedom and against the total industrialization of the planet. Like Columbus, we can believe the world is round and that our journey can bring us to land, or we can believe the world is flat and that we must sail off the edge. But, like Columbus, we must make the voyage to prove it. We will have to try to salvage a worldwide biome, a plant and animal community in which humans can vary and flourish, instead of conform and die. Certain ecologic notions must be widely understood. They run like a unifying thread through many portions of this book. Therefore they need a few pages to themselves.

The earliest concept in ecology was the food chain. A more recent one is the energy-budget. With these two concepts we can explore much of ecology and understand much of our world. What is a food chain and what has man done to it? What happens to energy-budgets when rural people move to town?

If we go back to the thin film of green plants which is the breathing lung of our planet and remember the vast expanse of natural forest or unbroken sod which existed so recently where man now lives, we can re-create for ourselves that earlier world. In the shadow of leaves, it is damp and cool, even in midsummer. On the floor of any forest walk thousands of creatures outside our lives, outside our sharp realities. Yet the sharpest reality of all is that we belong there, that this buffer protects us, these alien lives are necessary to our own.

Down through the spongy leaf mold of centuries rain and snow are filtered and collected again to run out in perennial springs, into brook or "crick" or lazy river. On our farm in Pennsylvania old rocks go back to the pre-Cambrian era—some of the oldest most deformed rocks in America that may have been uplifted several times over. Now they yield a steady flow of cold acid spring water through dry hot years or wet cold ones with no visible change. It takes years—160 or so of them—for the surface water to percolate down and flow into the springs. In our two-mile valley some sixty such springs edge to the surface along the swamp which is drained by a down-cutting brook. If we are thirsty we can kneel and pull away leaves and gravel and stir out the fine mud from a pocket no larger than a cup. Presently the water clears, the mud swirls gently away down a tiny rill and we can watch the sand grains being stirred and turned as the crystalline water brims up out of the ground. For enough to drink we must wait, and enough is never enough, so cold and pure it is. A spring, only thirty-five miles from the center of one of our largest cities, and pure enough to drink, never known to fail, hidden under leaves, priceless, forgotten! But only a cup at a time—not many creatures can drink there!

So long as water is near, plants and animals flourish. Plants protect the water source. Water is held in the valley by grace of root mat, by dense shade of maple and beech, by the forethought of some earlier farmer who replanted bands of pine and hemlock on the cropped-out hill. Plants are the bottom of the food chain, the spreading green subfloor of possibility for the herds of grazers, flocks of birds, hordes of nibbling insects. Higher animals have a far-from-simple food chain. What they eat as young creatures is not what they eat as adults. As young creatures they are often the prey of other animals. But the plant is everywhere the base. Something must eat the plant and convert it to the body tissue of animals. The primary grazers do this with special enzymes and organs for digesting the cellulose of leaf and stem. Here is the first clue to human ecology. Unlike the deer, the rabbit, the chicken, or the cow, man may survive on a diet of plants but not be fully nourished. He makes up the protein lack in his body by eating one of these primary grazers. He is carnivore as well as herbivore needing at least eggs, milk or cheese. Usually such a diet is supplemented by meat when he can get it. Desert peoples may bleed their male cattle rather than rob milk from the calves. Seacoast set-

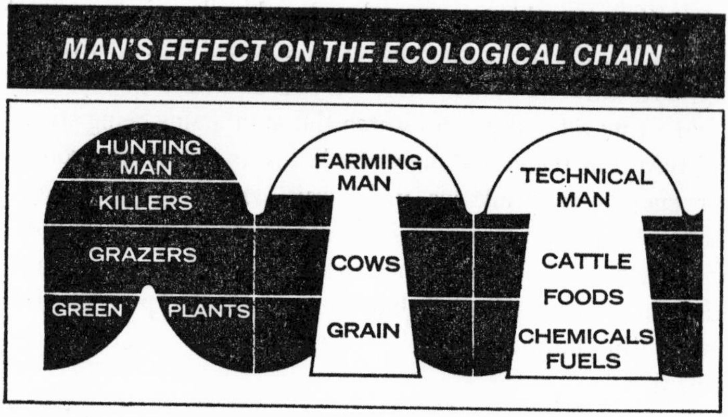

MAN'S EFFECT ON THE ECOLOGICAL CHAIN

HUNTING MAN
KILLERS
GRAZERS
GREEN PLANTS

FARMING MAN
COWS
GRAIN

TECHNICAL MAN
CATTLE
FOODS
CHEMICALS
FUELS

fig. 2

tlements may draw all protein requirements from shellfish or fish. But the primary fact is the same everywhere. Man needs food every day, and he needs animals to get it.

This primary fact of human ecology places man at the top of the food-chain pyramid. This pyramid diagrams quite simply the relation of animals grazing upon it to the basic green grass or the algae of the ocean. Large numbers and small size describe the lowest levels on land and sea: insects, mice and rabbits, plankton and herring. This numerous band is preyed upon by the level above them which has fewer mouths to feed. Finally, the eaters of flesh depend on the vast supply of herding animals, of flocking and schooling grazers for the quick energy of raw muscle. Man competes with the brotherhood of fang and claw, with stealthy panther and prowling wolf, with bear and tiger. Today, he even feels threatened by little fox and coyote. Man wants all the prey for himself; he grudges his brothers.

A natural environment supports a wide variety of birds, insects and mammals, all breeding and feeding and carrying out essential depredations upon each other. The balance of the total changes little from year to year unless there is an external disruption: a storm carries away the beach, a flood ruins the crop land or a tidal wave salts the meadow. Otherwise the community lives in a moving balance. Native plants and animals tend to flourish together.

About ten thousand years ago man ceased to be merely a hunter and food-gatherer. He not only settled down but he separated the domestic plants and animals from their wild relatives and under human protection displaced the natural communities. A vast increase of human numbers resulted. Wherever civilized man now lives he has a tendency to narrow and straighten the food chain. He concentrates upon the one or two key species he likes best or has found easy to raise. Because the human food chain requires animal protein, man has made severe inroads upon the native balance. He has reduced its variety over vast areas of the earth. Yet ecologists tend to measure the richness of a natural area in terms of the length and the variety of the food chains in it, and to gauge the stability of a community in terms of the many alternatives that are open to its members.

Man has reduced this richness and endangered this stability. Stream ecologists also measure the level of pollution in terms of the numbers and kinds of insect larvae, fish and protozoans killed out of the stream. In very basic ways, variety and health of a community go together. But man as the epidemic animal threatens both health and variety. Overcivilized, urban-raised people consider the impoverishment of city lot or city river a small loss. Only now we begin to recognize the great threat this is to human life, to human health and variety. In a nation where 70% of the people live in the orbit of cities, one of our great dangers is the dull acceptance of impoverished soil, polluted air, stinking waters, and the absence of natural species from our habitat. People can hardly legislate to protect a world they have never shared.

Who has seen a tiger swallowtail this last summer, or an osprey or an eagle? They went.

Perhaps it is not important, but it is more than a little spooky, for nothing we did made them go, nothing we knew of, nothing we cared about. And yet buried in the pages of *Silent Spring*, by Rachel Carson, published only in 1962, is the total prediction, the total fear. It is certain that knowledge is not helping us. Just because it exists we are not the less at risk. We have to use this knowledge soon enough, correctly enough, widely enough; and this means many more of us must come to understand ecology.

Recently modern medicine and sanitation have again jumped the population of human communities, not this time by reducing carnivores or increasing food but by wiping out internal predators or disease. For himself and for his favored plants and animals man combats on ever-widening fronts the molds, bacteria and virus which have arisen along with insects to threaten him. This new increase in numbers has the effect of putting a human mushroom cloud over the top of the food-chain pyramid. It was once successful for man to straighten the food chain. Why not again? To feed our newest increase we are proposing to culture algae, to eat grains, to substitute legume and nut protein for the milk, meat, cheese of previous peoples. In starving communities the domestic animal is a luxury few afford. Under such circumstances the cow is an inefficient converter of sunlight into milk. She must be over a year old to breed the first time. It is nine more months until the calf is dropped. She drops a good calf and gives a surplus of milk only if well fed. We must put a certain amount of energy into the cow in the form of food in order to get a certain level of production out again.

This brings us to the second notion in ecology which helps us to understand the relation of man to his food supply—the notion of energy-budget. We cannot upgrade energy systems without paying for it in energy. In poor areas of the world low-energy breeds of cattle survive with minimal diets and water supply. They have their place in a subsistence economy. The cow will produce a calf, a little milk and fat at low levels of energy input. She is not designed to make use of high-energy feeds. On the other hand, the high-producing breeds of Europe and North America have been made so by breeding and testing programs. Their records of fat and milk production depend on record inputs of high-energy feed. We cannot simply replace the scrub cattle of the developing countries by these high producers because high-energy feeds are not yet available. Without them, western cattle not only will not produce—they can hardly survive. If developing countries are able to produce a surplus of high-energy feeds, it will be equally wasteful to feed it to low-input local cows.

In certain parts of India continued cutting of the forest eventually led to its disappearance altogether. The land suffered loss of climate-tempering, soil-protecting forest patches. Animal chips then became the only source of fuel energy in wide areas. Only nomads or the most poverty stricken of farming regions burn cattle chips instead of returning them to the cropland. The effort to make such land support ever more people on the same sources of energy is the cause first of deforestation, and then of a steady decline in fertility.

In North India, this process has gone a very long way indeed. The blue haze of dung fires colors the early mornings. The brief coolness of dawn stirs the pungent sweet smoke along the ground. Chapati toasted over dung is delicious. Kerosene tastes ugly, electricity adds no flavor, and both must be purchased. Dung makes a dark fire, glowing red without flame. It makes the eyes sting and the throat struggle with homesickness. Like the birch fires of New England or the alder of the west, the distinctive local smoke tugs at deep memories, although today in most of New England the wood fire is a luxury, a symbol.

The poignance of the dung fire of India is its nearness to tragedy. There is no slack in this ecosystem. From rice and wheat straw comes the energy of buffalo and bullock. From the cattle comes the dung, gathered daily into baskets, dumped out to dry, patted by hand into large cakes baked in the sun. From the chips come the fires over which the village women cook rice or wheat. Like incense, the blue haze from the fires wisps upward in a final escape of energy from the system. The smoke is the only waste. At the edge of the village are stout round mounds, built of dried cakes, heavily thatched, fuel reserves for the long months of the monsoon.

Women since the dawn of time have provided the energy of muscle to keep the energy of hearth alive. In India they pat the dung or gather leaves, or they cut and carry home branches from the ever more distant patches on the hills. The dung fire will not be easily replaced. A perfected energy source, it is intertwined with the village patterns, with familiar pungence, with the taste of daily bread. Rice could be hulled, wheat could be ground into flour. But on the treeless plain, without the straw or the cattle or the blazing Indian sun there would be no dung cakes. Without the woman making something out of little, there would be no fire, no glowing red eye on which to cook the rice or the wheat.

We do not need to romanticize this village at the margin of death to realize how adapted it is. Its sparse pattern compresses human joy. Intellect hungers. But the whole industrial revolution could disappear without disturbing these villages of India.

Modern practices will conserve fertility and the tilth or living texture of the soil. Lime, potash, phosphorus and nitrogen will rebuild depleted land. But where is the energy-budget to come from? How are commercial fertilizers to reach the land that needs them, and who is to pay for them?

We know that the organic content of the soil can be increased without chemical fertilizers, by practices which turn under the trash of vines or straw, which plow down a green crop like soybeans or vetch, which rotate a row crop with the grasses of pasture or hay. But all these are expensive detours between the labor of planting and the business of eating. There must be latitude in the demand for food in order to sustain the best practices and to build up, instead of tear down, the soil. Trash-farming practices are well known but little followed, because of the energy loss involved. The simple walking plow of India is not adequate to the task of plowing down a green manure even if there were enough slack in food demand to permit a whole crop to be returned to the land. Man waits at the side of the field for the rice to be ripe, for wheat to darken, for soybeans to rattle and dry. At the end of the starving period he has just energy enough to bring in the harvest.

In earlier centuries northern peoples at the end of winter saved the last of their food, not for the weak, but for the strong, so they could fare forth and hunt for them in the return of spring.

The amount of energy creatures need to grow and mature, to migrate or to winter over determines the energy-budget of a population. Defense of territory cannot take too much energy from food-getting or it defeats the purpose.

In most species of birds nest-building and rearing of young are carried out when food supplies can be obtained with the minimum energy spent in hunting and catching. The late-nesting species which raise their young on seeds, like the goldfinches and siskins contrast sharply with the rodent-hunting hawks and owls who nest early and hunt while much of the meadow grass is still short and the woods still bare of leaves.

Energy-budgets are quite different for grazers and carnivores. The grazer must eat a large amount of relatively low-energy food and must spend the greater portion of each day eating and digesting. The carnivore obtains a much more concentrated food which releases energy into the bloodstream over a long period of time after eating. The carnivore spends the day in stalking and killing prey, but only a few minutes in devouring it.

When human families settled down, a larger energy-budget became available for productive tasks. Socializing the food-getting, child-rearing and shelter-building in a village enlarged the energy-budget for common undertakings and for the raising of children. But energy must be spent in getting food just the same. Instead of personally catching or growing food, man is now caught in a tight web of production and distribution systems over which he has no control and apart from which he can no longer survive.

We despise admitting this, but it is true.

We need gasoline and steel and commercial fertilizer in America, and packaging and preserving industries, and huge transportation systems to feed the present enlarged population concentrated in our cities. The clock cannot be set back. The whole species is vulnerable to any breakdown. A society which adopts a new energy-saving device quickly loses its option on the old. The optional nature of cars and tractors quickly disappeared, for although horses persisted for a brief time, their use steadily dwindled to nothing. Dependence on the new item had been created. Agriculture which moves away from ancient land patterns and practices can rarely go back. We cannot revert to a range economy for livestock; the range is gone. We cannot revert to a henyard economy for egg production; the demand is far too great.

The energy needed to make land produce a surplus is too easily neglected in talking about farming. But it spells all the difference. Neither as serfs nor as comrades of the revolution have the Russian peasants been able to produce on a par with the small landholders of Western Europe. Naked authority cannot make a man productive. On the farm, men work best for their own families, their own table, their own profit from surplus left to sell. Where landholding is handed down, and the level of existence not too low, the owner will husband field and forest. He is the best assurance of good farming practices the land can have. But city-minded, wage-minded, factory-conscious planners overlook the essential surge of extra energy that the whole farm family pours into production at planting and harvest time. In America, eighteen and twenty hours are not unusual in the peak months. Today both in Israel and Russia—as different as two societies can be in politics, aims, and origins—private farm holdings are outproducing communal farms, and are spelling the critical difference between enough and not enough for free markets in nearby towns. The very same people cannot mobilize themselves to the same kind of effort on communal lands.

In America, industrial farming cuts all corners, uses all machinery and mass purchase and sale techniques. But the land suffers. Our rivers are sterilized with pesticides in the name of efficiency and progress. Long-term conservation practices are not guaranteed continuity from land sale to land sale. Profits from such enterprises are not coming chiefly from the land, but from money management, tax devices and subsidy payments. Business managers can manipulate money but not the long-term fertility of the land. Ideally the long-term tilth and fertility of the soil should be protected. No single generation should be able to exploit it for quick profit, or deplete it over the short run.

To get grains to market, the farmer shortens the food-chain in part of his enterprise. But we should be very careful how extensively or permanently we encourage this. In grain agriculture the tilth and future of the soil is at stake. We know that the Mayans outran their corn economy, and that tropical soils once bared to rain and sun soon lose the richness of centuries. The key ions, potassium and phosphate, are in total use in the tropics each year. There is no surplus for a crop. Each crop cuts into the supply. Unless the excrement from crop users returns to that soil, that local cycle is demolished forever. Modern agriculture has not found a way to protect tropical soil from sun and rain even though fertilizers may seem to offset at first the steady removal of crops from the land.

The orange groves of California suggest even in temperate zones that steady fertilizing is not enough. After thirty years, size and hardiness and yield are shrinking on the irrigated land. Salts are piling up at the interface of soil and subsoil. The new techniques to resolve the problem are not here as yet.

In California, no one will starve without oranges. But modern irrigation has gone abroad to lands where hunger presses and the energy-budget is tight. In the sixties, the Indus River was diverted into a great irrigation grid. Joyously food was produced in the desert, but in less than a decade of use, the irrigated lands became mineralized. The brief increase of productivity was lost. Food from the desert proved a costly mirage.

We suspect from historical records that the Middle East was once a much greener land, reduced first to grain and then to desert over centuries of cropping. We recognize that the dust bowl of America in the thirties which started the wanderings of the Okies and the Arkies began not on any one farm or in any one dooryard, but in all of them.

Breaking the prairie sod and plowing it for wheat promised a cash crop which made some men rich and beckoned to the greed in others. The root mat of the prairie grass is thick and tough and resists the action of winds even in the dry years.

The winds blew over the fiery plains and tore at the tough mat for centuries before the white man came and burned it off and then broke it with his tractor or huge teams of mules and his plow. The sod went, and the grain came, leaving the soil without any protection but the thin stolons of wheat. The sod went and the land went after it and after the land blew into dunes around the barnyard and up against the fences, the people went, loaded into cars, staggering onto trains, walking, leaving the land whose ecosystem they had never understood, had raped and destroyed in the most terrible innocence, the innocence of not knowing.

Could anyone have told those dust-bowl farmers not to plant wheat? Could anyone have told them to interplant, to intergraze, to cover the soil with trash crops, to plant windbreaks? Not until too late—not until afterward.

The energy-budget necessary to reclaim that land is out of all proportion to that needed to protect it in the first place. So the ecology of man is the ecology of the land, of where he lives and gets his living. There are short cuts he cannot take; there are detours he can neglect only at the peril of his children. It is easy now to look at the history of the dust bowl, at the soil maps and the rainfall maps and wonder why they did not know, did not see what they were doing. But the fact is that they did not see. It is pretty certain today, in our haste to dam rivers, to use chemical fertilizers and weed controls and pesticides, and to bypass animals in the food chain, that we do not know what we are doing either. It looks as though we are going to find out—afterward.

Natural Selection

8

NOWHERE in nature is the lazy bird or squirrel rewarded by living offspring. Nowhere is the careless fish or rabbit rewarded by forgiveness. He is knapped off by the first hungry predator. The price of survival in the wild is vigilance and conformity. The least disobedient wriggle of the small rabbit and the fox has a dinner! One unwary leap of the trout for a midge along the pond edge, and the osprey has a fish sailing home in his talons. Constantly enforced cruelty is the price of the beauty and variety we see—and the harmony we feel—when we walk through the meadows and observe the interactions of creatures.

This is not the kind of selection nice people like to notice among living things. Nor do they like to face up to the fact that human beings take part in such choices. Nor do they admit the duty of selecting one human over another in spite of the fact that all social life is carried on by just such selections, and always has been.

Natural selection operates upon a breeding population by selecting those adults who will produce the next breeding population. It operates upon all the weak links of the human chain; upon the embryo which can die before birth, upon the infant which dies in childbirth, upon the infant which dies before a year. It operates in less obvious ways to reduce the fertility of the couple and to reduce the fertility of their children. In human societies this can occur in many ways, from mumps and gonorrhea, to the social forms of infertility ascribed to bachelors and spinsters and religious celibates.

The ability of a plant or animal to survive can be developed in two opposite directions. One direction is to increase the tolerance it may have for changes in its environment. The other is to intensify its special adaptations to unique conditions. Plants and animals which are selected *for* in favorable conditions, may be severely selected *against* when conditions change.

In a temperate valley, the plants and animals will adapt to survive continuous change, from dry hot weather to cold wet weather, wind and snow. But no plant in the valley will be as adapted to snow as the edelweiss of the Alps or to dryness as the Joshua tree of the desert, nor to wind as the firs of the seaward islands. The generally adapted grouse can survive in a snowdrift but will not compare to the penguin in adaptation to cold.

The generalized temperate zone peoples will not survive either the arctic or the tropics as well as tribes specially adapted to extreme conditions. Living in those conditions is made easier by stable genetic patterns, which become a type, and eventually dominate the given population through breeding success. People living within such a local type help fix it by further social selection and group approvals. Today, as we grow up out of our own local communities, and move around in the world we become aware that the many different kinds of hair, shapes of eyes, width of nose, length of limbs, color of skin are part of such genetic patterns. Interesting in themselves, and perhaps useful, these are markers of other differences inherited along with them which have had adaptive value.

Among animals, such signs of difference provide recognition systems, which may be sexual cues, or may trigger hostility and avoidance. The albino robin is chased by his own kind as well as more easily stalked by predators. Among human populations today, natural fear and distrust greet many of our visible differences. Under new conditions of crowding, fear and violence triggered by visible difference between Hindu and Moslem, Malay and Chinese, black and white are wiping out whole families and ethnic units. We cannot abolish visible difference. We cannot very well live in separate enclaves and carry on the work of the industrial world. Once, fear and violent reactions may have been advantageous. But today, the bearer of these reactions is now at greater risk from other kinds of men. We do not tend to think of our own behavior patterns as a factor in natural selection. But differences in behavior have always meant to the rabbit and the fish and the human the difference between life and sudden death.

For man or any other animal to become adapted to special conditions through selection, those conditions must have remained constant over a number of generations. There must have been enough genetic variety in the population for selection to work upon. Useful change is believed to accumulate only slowly, within a stable pattern of genetic linkages. Until human culture appeared on the scene of evolution, the only way advantage could spread was through production of offspring carrying an advantageous gene. It was a naive breeding advantage and nothing more which produced the present complex forms of life. Each successive advantage led to the next, so that the animal's ability and his structure improved stepwise together.

Humans have shortened the process. They communicate advantages; they do not have to breed them in. But selection is involved in it just the same. The discovery of fire, of the wheel, of gunpowder altered all subsequent life. People who had them temporarily triumphed over people who did not. Man burned the prairies to corner his game. He survived the ice. He rolled across the far horizon. He decimated man and animal. In biology, as in a murder case, we are always unraveling the sequence of events, deciding what happened together, and trying to fix special dates in history. There is no point where we can say here man appeared. We do not know if fire was discovered, and lost again, once or many times. Currently the human dwelling places where evidence of hearths appeared go back to the early Pleistocene, roughly one and three-quarter million years ago. Without date is the still earlier origin of language. We only know from the cave drawings of the Pyrenees that man was well acquainted with symbols before the glaciers disappeared.

Now computers have given societies who have them a murderous advantage over those who haven't. Yet in many physical ways we hardly differ at all from the first men who attempted to divine the future from ashes or entrails, or from the conjunction of stars. Side by side with the computer print-out we are still staring into ashes and studying the conjunction of planets for clues to the human future. We have known about the clues of evolution, natural selection and ecologic balance for only a short time. Yet we are as young and as old as the songbirds—whose songs and migrations have rivaled our own, and yet have been so different. We prefer to think of ourselves as one species; although many of our languages and cultural patterns have developed in breeding isolation. In the same period of time, by intense selection the birds have fragmented into many hundreds of species unable to interbreed, constantly shifting their ranges, expanding and contracting with fluctuations of climate and plant cover. What has selected the songbirds for extremes of speciation? What has selected us to prevent speciation?

We do not know. Human willingness to mate across large visible differences may have been one decisive factor. Sexual attraction is constantly occurring between members of very different races. Unopposed, such a tendency would have mixed up our gene pools quite thoroughly. However in many societies selection runs strongly against the children of couples who breed across sharp racial lines. This counterpressure maintains our genetically distinct races and subraces. Human populations have expanded rapidly before. Some have been able to adapt their behavior to new levels of crowding because crowding in itself offers protection against enemies, and advantages in trade. For others, crowding placed a fatal strain upon food-raising or led to fatal outbreaks of disease. Psychological responses to crowding vary from migration and subfertility to the bizarre human sacrifices in the Yucatan at the end of the Mayan empire. The seemingly wanton killing of surrendered peoples which occurs so often in accounts of invading armies may be a very basic "make-room" reaction.

Genetic difference between populations, and historic accidents provide levers for natural selection. Within each population, genetic difference between families also gives rise to selection. But no advantage carries over into the next generation unless there is successful reproduction and the trait recurs.

Sometimes the trait which most affects an individual is a trait of his population and not of his own person. In 1930, a low birth rate, in 1946 a high birth rate had serious if not overriding impact on all American babies born in those years. The cohort—all persons born in the same year—is an important entity which can be followed from birth to death. Each cohort will have its own characteristics and may experience very different conditions from cohorts just a few years older or younger.

The young fox born on the crest of vole abundance can hunt a narrow territory and will have no trouble supplying kits with food. The vixen will be smooth and silky and produce good milk. Other foxes will den not far away and they can be heard barking at each other on a moonlight night. The young fox born a year or two later, after voles have declined steeply, will find food scarce. He must range far, and drive other foxes away. His vixen is poor and kits are hard to raise. Hunger encourages disease, especially in the harsh months. The fox pair able to raise the most young under these adversities will dominate the oncoming population of foxes, while the cohort into which their young are born will be greatly reduced. During years of scarcity, skillful stalking and hunting is required. In intervals of abundance, populations increase and selection is relaxed. Even the lazy fox can raise a family. Periodic winnowing of genetic stock occurs in this way to many species. Blizzards, ice storms, fire and flood, failure of staple food, inroads of a new competitor all provide occasions for natural selection. Now one, now another set of traits will prove adapted, now one species, now another will survive disaster and will expand its percentage of the total population after the disaster recedes.

We desire favorable conditions of life and social equalities for everyone. But we need to realize that these are just the conditions which encourage deselection in the animal kingdom, which lead to population explosion, and set the stage for winnowing by a new disaster.

Humans respond like the fox to sudden new food supply. In 1695 in Ireland, the population was slightly over one million. The potato was introduced from the Americas. In 1821 population was above 6.8 million—a remarkably rapid upswing. Then potato blight struck without warning. A fungus black-rotted the tubers in storage, killed the plants in the field. A million or more people starved. Millions emigrated. Among the remnant, the birth rate fell. At this time, Irish cohorts only ten years apart experienced very different fates and selection pressures. Cohorts born in the same decade differed in size by more than 50 %. Who survived to become the modern Irish? Who went overseas? Who died? These are haunting demographic questions, questions of natural selection.

The potato also went to Nepal from British India. There it has become a favorite food above the 9,000-foot level in Sherpa country. In spite of living conditions as severe as any in the world, a fourfold increase in population resulted. So far the blight has not followed.

On the smaller scale of town and family, two or three successive cohorts may show wildly different size. Sometimes the same local families survive and retain prominence. Sometimes the leadership is entirely swept away. Each such upheaval offers new handles to selection.

Some are grim.

Into an affluent, influential and numerous community came the 1935 cohort of native-born German Jews. Death and migration scattered them and the community into which they were born.

The cohorts now being born around the world are the largest ever known. Each secure, distinct, genetically isolated community is thinking only of itself; of its right to be parents and its joy in children. But for the children, the size of their cohort is overriding. It measures the demand upon food and water, jobs and housing, medicine and sanitation which they will take part in twenty-five years from now.

As populations approach the very small family, selection pressures will intensify. Your neighbor has to raise fifteen children to have 50% more than you with ten. Between a family of ten and a family of eleven the difference is only 10%. But when you have two children, your neighbor has to have only one more child to have 50% more than you. If you have one child, and he has two, the difference is 100%. These facts which enter into human selection enter into our fears and antagonisms too. Formerly in our empty world, they led to expansion and breeding races. Today, under conditions of crowding, the intractable nature of these facts is the best of reasons for everyone to stop at two.

Human Selection

9

ALTHOUGH THE THEORY of evolution was supported by fossil evidence, and by the work of plant and animal breeders, how selection took place and what structures it took place in had received only vague answers before 1900. Gregor Mendel's precise work with peas had shown the segregation of inherited traits and their independent assortment in the offspring. He gave the first mathematical base to inheritance. Thomas Hunt Morgan in his work with drosophila gave Mendel's traits a locus as genes on the chromosomes of the cell. Later on J. D. Watson and F. H. C. Crick (1953) gave exactitude to the gene model and located it precisely in the DNA helix of the chromosome in the nucleus of the cell. Because of this work, the model of evolution is clearer today. Its history can be measured by radioactive dating of fossils, by calculations of gene mutation rates, and rates of gene spread. Its chemical and cellular base is beginning not only to be known but is subject to increasingly sophisticated manipulation and prediction.

At each crisis in the genetic history of living material the odds that a new genetic response would prove fatal were enormous. Vast numbers of extinct forms attest to this fact. The genetic material living on earth today is the most improbable survivor of endless accidents of climate and radiation and cellular event.

The proteins which have carried on this evolutionary process repeat themselves from one generation to the next in complex chains of definite pattern. The units which make up the patterns are amino acids. Strung along the chromosome on a skeleton of sugar and phosphate, the sequence of acids accounts for the inherited differences that have occurred in the past, that occur today; and from these must come the difference of the future.

In such a chemical structure, restrictions and possibilities go hand in hand. Radical change of geometric shape would disarray whole patterns and lead to radical changes of chemical activity, to sharp mutation and to lethal outcomes. The extraordinary forms of life shifting over long periods of time present a memorable pattern of endless, unpredictable change. Yet at any one time, the living race of plant or animal is genetically quite stable. Considerable resistance to further physical evolution is embedded in chromosomes of modern species. The chromosome has one unanswerable weapon which defends existing systems. It fails to copy a change that is too great. This is a security and a danger to modern humans. For we ourselves with atomic blasts and contaminated foods threaten changes to the chromosome that *are* too great. The atmosphere which makes the green lung possible, which gives us oxygen and moisture, also screens out most of the lethal radiation coming from the sun. It cannot protect us from what we ourselves produce.

Natural diets include compounds with genetic action, without our knowing it, but not in the massive amounts and universal distributions of modern pesticides and drugs. The ongoing genetic material is protected in its stability by relatively frail defenses very delicately maintained within the cell. The device of dying if threatened is the extreme protection. A cell can die; it can fail to divide; it can divide incorrectly. Scientists fear the unaccustomed exposure of genetic material. It may be easy to ruin our genetic stability by such exposures, to create lethals and to cause mass sterility, perhaps not of ourselves but of our important plant and animal resources. Scientists studying cells and genetic defects are deeply concerned lest our great triumphs of technology prove fatal.

Few of us stop to question the famed "perfection" of the forward-looking human eye. But it is a classical example of natural selection and human deselection. We cannot imagine the tedium with which its first slow development took place. Once begun, improved forward vision led to greater natural survival and was rapidly selected for. To begin, there must have been a range of lateral eye positions like that of the fish, for selection to work upon. The socket must have been shifted forward and numerous veins and nerves modified together with the muscles at each generation of forward shift. Each slight advantage had to spread widely enough through the population to permit breeding to pass it on. Selection must have worked upon many faulty models before the primate forward-looking eye was perfected. In developing the eye, the simian habit of swinging from one branch to another at great speed was one selector. Hunting was another. The most accurate survived, and had the most offspring.

Today, the perfected ability to gauge distance at high speed now permits us to merge into thruway traffic above seventy miles an hour. But selection is an ongoing process. Some time ago in human history our precise stereo vision became infiltrated with an apparently dominant genetic defect, hereditary myopia or nearsightedness. In modern society, selection against this defect does not take place because eye glasses correct it adequately. Nearsighted people survive very well. However, if the nearsighted had to merge onto the modern thruway without glasses, they would be selected against instantly—as instantly as the monkey who missed a branch in the tropical tree tops. Vast numbers of the human race have already lost the perfection of human sight. This has occurred through a new genetic defect and social deselection. This example of the eye makes clear what we have not been willing to realize—our own responsibility as agents in human deselection—the impact of ourselves upon ourselves.

By many inventions we now interfere with the inroads of disease. We offset the inherited disabilities of nearsightedness, diabetes, mental deficiency and many other weaknesses of the species. The winnowing by an exposed life no longer occurs.

More subtle, but equally vital, the toolmaker no longer has to improvise. No longer does each male child have to develop levers and pulleys to save his own back, to outsmart the exhausting forces of nature. Systems engineering and manufacturing does this for him. Tool-using and toolmaking ability is not demanded from the ordinary run of modern men. In earlier societies, the developed skills of language belonged to leaders of all communities. They orated, sang sagas and gave down oracles and commandments. Writing increased the basic power of language, giving it duration from one place to another, and from age to age. Modern communications media have altered the power of language. The ordinary masses of mankind now neither have to master the task of expressing themselves, nor the task of grasping the thought process of their leadership. All they have to grasp is the end result, the one-syllable word decisions in the TV picture. The great human enterprise of thought and language can pass them by. It is not necessary for more than a few to learn to calculate. Ordinary people do not have to spell. Life no longer depends upon the quick grasp of new situations, the quick transmission of clear signals, or wise orders to action. These skills will not be practiced. Qualities which once let one man excel over another no longer have selective advantage. The large brain came from tool-using and language-using. Sharp eyes, strong bodies, healthy birth, intelligent decisions produced the original human stock. Now, for better or worse, most of the effects of modern human culture reverse the trend of selection. Yet today we concede that inherited behavior patterns were adaptive; we admit genetic traits are levers which selection is acting upon to produce the next generation.

In the course of evolution, humans have picked up many harmful mutant genes. They have had to pay for another class of protective genes by withstanding quite severe levels of genetic disadvantage inherited along with them. The bearers of clearly disadvantageous genes reproduce at the rate the gene itself permits. There has been neither the knowledge nor the means to interfere. The classic case of this kind is achondroplasia or dwarfism studied in Denmark, where in certain towns quite remarkable records go back for two or more centuries. These have taught us much about the rate of natural gene mutation in a given population.

We know that this famous defect of dwarfism so depresses the number of offspring who live to grow up and breed that dwarfism would disappear from the population in a few generations, except that the genetic accident which caused it in the first place recurs at a definite rate. New dwarfs arise at this rate in each generation. It is as though certain gene loci were accident prone, although we do not yet know what the specific accident is.

We can compute the mutation rate if we first compare the number of normal sisters and brothers to the number of dwarf siblings. Then we compare the numbers of children born to normal siblings with the number born to dwarfs. From the first ratio of dwarfs to their brothers and sisters, we calculate a relative frequency for the dwarf gene in the population. The second ratio, between sets of offspring, measures the depressant effect of being dwarf upon having children. There are more parent dwarfs than children born to them. The difference between the two ratios gives the rate at which this gene mutates into the population to maintain dwarfs.

$$\frac{\text{dwarfs}}{\text{normal siblings}} - \frac{\text{dwarf children}}{\text{sibling children}} = \text{mutation rate}$$

Most defects as severe as dwarfism prevent reproduction altogether. Dwarfism is unusually visible. Therefore it was recorded early and accurately. Dwarfs found sheltered niches like the circus and the medieval court where, in spite of the selection pressure against them, they found mates and earned a livelihood. Even so, the embittered writings left behind by famous dwarfs hardly make us want to increase their numbers.

Among the white population of western Europe and North America, mongolism is the most widespread mental defect. So far no preventive measure exists. Extensive profiles of parents producing this defect in their offspring have shown us no way to predict it. There is a high but not perfect correlation with age of the mother at conception of the defect. The tendency of the mother to produce a mongol is probably an inherited trait. Because mongols can occur with a normal twin, the defect seems to be an accident to that particular maternal egg. Like most other human ills, mongolism shows a range of severity. The less severely afflicted can and do produce offspring at a reduced rate. If we have taken these children on our knee and hugged them, if we have dealt with their excitable ways, and their doglike affection, it is incredible that we let them get pregnant or become the parent of a normal child.

Sickle cell presents us with even more of a conundrum in social decision, because here we are dealing with a gene which confers both positive and negative effects. In the single or heterozygotic state, it confers valuable protection against malaria. Sickle cell is believed to have come to the United States from those parts of Africa with highly fatal forms of malaria, and is found only in persons of African ancestry. For the individual who suffers from sickle-cell anaemia, the effect is all bad; but for his brothers or sisters with only one gene for this condition, there was a long-established advantage.

Malaria is caused by the plasmodium parasite transmitted through the bite of a mosquito. The parasite develops in human liver cells, multiplies there, bursts, thousands escaping into the human blood stream. The tiny zoites seek a red blood cell, enter it, mature into a score of new cells and escape again.

Parasites of this next generation also seek blood cells. This cyclic pattern gives malaria its typical spikes of pain and fever. In the midst of other concerns one can pause to wonder how the mosquito-plasmodium-human systems co-adapted to keep this disease at a relatively high level among most of the tropical peoples of the world. The sickle gene affects the red blood cell causing it to look sickle-shaped under the microscope. Recent studies show more of this condition than previously suspected. The disease comes to medical attention because it causes serious illness whenever a child receives the sickle gene from both parents. Resulting anaemia can be so severe that the untreated child dies long before reproducing age. Even with treatment, sickle-cell anaemia is a miserable, usually fatal disease. One eighteen-year-old patient had a record of 108 admissions to the hospital, which fails to measure his sufferings from injections or the disability caused by this disease.

This high mortality of the double dose would have caused the gene to die out of the population except for one thing: malarial parasites do not flourish in sickle cells. Received from one parent only, the single dose of sickle cell protects the child against severe malaria. There is some reduction in the capacity of the blood to carry oxygen, but this disadvantage is slight compared to the risk of death from malaria in bad years or in bad localities. The difference in risk is enough to give sickle children an advantage in survival which has caused the gene to stabilize at high levels in many tropical countries. Where pressure has been most severe, the gene frequency of sickle cell has attained 40% of the population. In malarial areas the usual level is 20%. When pressure from malaria is removed, the gene frequency might be expected to drift below 10%.

This is a beautifully adaptive system, which is being altered by modern science, and by human parents, who are concerned about their personal role in carrying this gene. If a carrier-parent mates with another carrier, each child would run a 25% risk of receiving the fatal double dose; each child would run a

50% chance of receiving the sickle gene from one parent and a normal from the other, and only a 25% chance of receiving two normal genes. How often this situation occurs depends upon the frequency of the gene in the total population likely to mate.

Harmful dominant genes like dwarfism will not accumulate in the population as fast as a recessive lethal like sickle cell. This sounds strange. In dominance, the gene does pass to 75% of the children. Only 25% will have the double dose and die young or before birth. Fifty per cent will have one gene only but they will also *show* the trait and be selected against. The final 25% will be double recessive and clear of the gene. In dominance, selection works not only against the lethal double dose, but also against whatever visible disadvantage—being dwarf, for example—is carried by the single gene. The 50% of children who have the single gene are dwarf. They will have fewer offspring and more difficulty in raising them than normal individuals.

On recessive lethals like sickle cell the selective force acts differently. The single-dose gene is sheltered from selection because it travels in disguise. The trait is not dominant, and does *not show* in the mixed offspring. The sickle cell carrier does not suspect it unless clinical work on his family has suggested it to him. He has no visible reason not to marry and have children. If the trait has been an advantage to him in malaria, or it proves so for his children, he will not suspect that either. A gene like this can spread quite rapidly through a relatively closed breeding unit.

The population in which this trait occurs ought to set priorities. Infants with sickling disease used to die. How much medical energy do parents want exerted to prevent their death? We can rush out and save sickle cell babies, but probably to the sorrow of the baby and the disadvantage of the future breeding population. One child with this defect which the community saves and does not prevent from breeding can lead to many more such children it must also save. When malaria is absent even a single dose of sickle cell is a disadvantage, appearing as a chronic anaemia. Natural selection developed this long-run adaptation to malaria. It certainly seems cruel in the short run and callous to the individual. To prevent the suffering of many future children, to protect a population, human programs may also have to be severe in the short run, and firm with individuals.

Genetic diabetes is increasing because insulin and its modern analogues protect these patients through childbearing. Fortunately, so long as our social protections are intact, they can be valuable and happy citizens. We can treat them. In a disruptive natural or unnatural disaster, this vulnerable population would not make it. Why then encourage or permit them to expand their numbers? From these examples it is clear that humans are now selecting other humans. Our actions are producing effects with consequences for everyone whether we like it or not.

The dilemma of medical selection is clearly understood only by a few population biologists and younger physicians. Yet the *acts* of selection are carried out every day by a medical community which is still largely unscientific in point of view. Physicians fail to realize that not making a decision on selection is still selective.

We all approve of protecting the human race—until it comes down to doing it. If we set out to mow the meadow, we know very well that mowing favors short clover and desirable grasses by preventing tall weeds from going to seed. But as we go out the gate to mow the meadow, we raise the cutter bar. It will not mow anything at all. Life is sacred! Who are we to mow the weeds!

Our language is at fault, not our human ability to judge. We judge humans all the time. We make all kinds of decisions when we wish: to fight, to die, to imprison, to put others to death. Such decisions are made on the merits of the case in the social context. Of course they may be either right or wrong. But in these areas the remark, "Life is sacred" does not paralyze us, even when we agree with it. When we ask, under what circumstances must it be saved, then we are getting down to the practical language of action and choice.

Mowing favors the pasture. Not mowing favors the weeds. Nothing we do or refuse to do is neutral. Today, the context of every family is a crowded world. There are enough people already. Against such a background, and remembering that life is sacred, we must ask, "Is the risk of defect real? Then give a good reason to risk it for a new baby, rather than adopt a child who needs you!"

Recognized defects are one place to begin to apply the same standards of selection and judgment we have applied so long to cats and dogs and house plants. It is a real disregard of life to refuse to make these judgments.

Humanists have said that we do not know enough about human genetics to make such decisions. As a scientific statement perhaps this is true. But today this statement is being used as a rule for inaction, which has a definite genetic impact of its own. Formerly, doing nothing was not committing us to any result we could predict with certainty beforehand. Now we can indeed predict adverse results from doing nothing. In genetic counseling, because of population pressure upon every decision, the pendulum has swung from live and let live, to let die, or prevent from being born.

Death Control Is in Control

10

SUDDENLY WE REALIZE that the increase in the world's people is not voluntary. We have had nothing to say about the advances in medicine or technology which cause us to live longer and to produce more of our kind. Scientists themselves find nothing voluntary about their work or their discoveries. Once DDT or Salk vaccine or penicillin were discovered, they were fated to be used. Death control is in control. We must snatch the short-term benefits, and rejoice over them, regardless of the long-term consequences. Whether wise or not, we respond to the nearest threat. We rush out to attack the mosquito or bacteria most directly threatening us—and nothing in our genetic bones warns us to pull back from the awesome risk our poisons have become. Nothing warns us to pull back from our own unchecked productivity. We have no instincts to make us sense these new kinds of danger.

Modern techniques are not really controlling nature. They are merely tipping the ancient balance temporarily in our favor. Today we pride ourselves on our scientific ability to save ourselves and our kind. We take joy in it. No choice there! When the pendulum swings back, as it is already beginning to in the sudden drug resistance of insects, molds, and bacteria, we will blame the cruelty of nature. Nothing voluntary about it!

The atom bomb is the least voluntary of our discoveries. Not even the men inventing it could pull back from its fearsome prospects; men who knew better than any of us its dimensions of risk for us all. The notion of overkill applies not only to the mythical enemy on the drawing board but also and inexorably to ourselves. Each year that passes without further use of atomic weapons deepens the uncertainty over our future actions. Have we passed the danger point? Are we sure the bomb will never be used in anger? Or does each advancing year and advance of knowledge bring us closer to that terrible event? We do not know! We do know that we cannot seem to stop producing and deploying these ultimate weapons, which we hope will never be used.

In a world with overkill threatening us, overbirth seems a natural, even an acceptable and necessary response. This happens in many threatened animal species pressing against some limiting factor like space or food. The lemmings endure overbirth and overkill, cyclically, nothing voluntary about it. This is what the complacent demographers mean when they say calmly the population problem will take care of itself. It certainly will, unless we take care of it!

In our barns, we are very practical about the lives of the animals that serve us, even those we keep for pleasure, and cling to with affection. Our decisions are dispassionate ones, based upon cost versus benefit. We make every effort to prevent disease and accident. We make very little effort in treatment. Once abortion begins, we do little to save the calf; it would be weak anyhow. We do little to raise the deformed or the premature, because its foods and its care subtract from that of more profitable animals. In the barn, the overall energy-budget strictly controls death control. But not in the hospital! We take heroic measures in treatment there. Threatened abortion mobilizes emergency wards whose personnel never stop to think that abortion is a natural control over frail mothers or defective embryos. In the drive to save life, we never consider that perhaps the mother should lose this infant and start over. For humans in a hospital there is no control of modern death control—not the wisdom of the doctor, the wish of the parent, nor the need of society.

In the premature nursery, the priorities of our strange medical system are most askew. While healthy babies go home without a prospect of future health care, or even a sufficient diet, costs in the premature nursery run many times higher than for the infant of normal birth weight. Often serious malformations caused the prematurity in the first place. Intelligence may be lowered, general resistance is less. Yet by heroic measures these scraps of humanity are preserved to bring their parents not only certain debt, but uncertain handicaps throughout their joint lives. Every doctor, every nurse has watched the reckless saving of disasters, and has had to aid in the upsidedownness of these acts. When medicine was not so effective, it saved many useful individuals from marginal troubles. Now it is so skillful that it can save almost anything that breathes, and too often it does. There is nothing voluntary about this. The old ironclad public morals covering the medical profession have not yet shifted to control of life instead of control of death.

Only twenty-five years of death control on the superior scale of modern medicine has brought life to the brink of disaster. We have not merely saved individual infants in hospitals in expensive suburbia. But we have saved them by the epidemic-full in poverty-stricken villages around the world. The use of new vaccines in old countries has halved infant mortality. In the forties, malaria fell before DDT. Then we went after these same countries with smallpox vaccination. Now we are following up with measles vaccine and triple shots for tetanus, diphtheria and whooping cough. Impressive is that great preventer of living tragedy, polio vaccine! No doubt about it, the control of death and reduction of misery made modern western medicine look marvelous in the first years of its benefits. Children lived. Crippling decreased. Men and women once debilitated by malaria were able to work again. But also to breed!

About life control, in all innocence, or deliberately, we did nothing.

The results have been sad for everyone. In nations receiving medical aid, growth rates have doubled just as demand for education and better living burgeoned. New babies placed a much heavier burden upon the working parents. More mouths to feed did not mean more food. In countries that subsisted in the forties, serious hunger is stalking now. The famines predicted for the end of the century are grim probabilities. The green revolution is a popular fraud, buying at best a little more time; at worst turning deluded peoples away from control of births.

To the western countries, the failure of modern medicine to produce healthy and happy populations is a bitter blow. Our naive programs expected birth rates to fall as far in a generation as ours have fallen over three hundred years. Now we know. Birth rates in Egypt and India, in South America and Africa are not falling. Yet we continue the same death control as before. We are unbalancing even more rapidly new areas of the world. Although Americans proudly send the S.S. *Hope* to other countries to teach death control, no birth control techniques are taught. Sanitation, insect vector control, the germ theory of infection are "gifts" of western science and medicine to the rest of the world. They are bitter gifts. Along with skills which control death, even now we export a medical-legal morality which inhibits life control. In South Korea, which has always accepted infanticide, abortion and sale of children, American aid attempts to forbid these natural responses to poverty. We are forcing our mores upon a very old ecology.

So long as medicines and vaccines and techniques save life, we praise ourselves and play God by interfering with natural events. But we put the lights out and depart from the stage when we cannot save lives. We refuse to decide whom to let die quietly and whom to prevent from being born.

Fortunately for the world, Asia is more practical than the

west. Foreign physicians are coming to their senses. Some of them are ready to resist our aid for measures which reduce infant mortality, unless and until women have access to birth control and the population is declining beforehand. The westerner strenuously objects to this stern compassion claiming that unless infant deaths drop first, women will not use birth control. Of course not, if this is the carefully publicized opinion!

In a beautiful small country, one leader said to me, "We are the toughest people in the world. We can survive anything." When I looked surprised, he explained grimly, "We have to be tough. We have one of the highest infant mortalities in the world."

He went on to explain that food was just then ample. Nourishment was good. He hoped to develop education, birth control, and food reserves, letting sickness take care of itself. His humanity is tough-minded. Births and deaths are in balance around 40/1000. But teams of rescue from the soft nations, from UNESCO, and the United Nations, and Great Britain, and the U.S., want to rush in there and save babies. We are outsiders who give no thought to the energy-budget of such a change, to whether capacity exists to sustain more people or finance such programs. We give no thought to the value of stern selection for the individual who must survive a rugged life.

To be kind in cruel ways, to be cruel in kind ways—we shall have to face up to this confusion in aid programs all over the world. Or very quickly there will be no aid to give, even to ourselves!

"People cannot be selected like cattle!" is the outraged cry.

They work harder than cattle in many countries. They cannot be shot when they get too old to work. They cannot be sent to market when they fail to earn. They cannot be killed and used for leather when there is no fodder. People cannot be selected for shape or strength or healthiness. They cannot be selected for their ability to bear strong young easily. They cannot expect scientifically balanced feed, or dry barns and clean straw. We certainly cannot treat people like cattle!

For millions of people alive in the world, and being born into it at three per second, it is too bad they can't be treated like cattle.

When the barn is full, the careful herdsman sends his poorest animals down the road to market. But when the human barn is full, it overflows into the yard until everyone is equally crowded and miserable, diseased and underfed. The great humanitarian health programs are going to prove great humanitarian blunders. Our good intentions will not let us escape blame or self-blame, or the crescendo of consequences.

There is nothing sacred about life as women are being forced to lead it in many parts of the world. But this does not stop them from producing children, if the society is placing pressure upon them. Social pressure is clear when we look at the deliberate production of known defects like haemophilia (bleeder's disease). Only one chance in four exists for a son of a carrier-mother to be normal. Each daughter has a fifty-fifty chance of being a carrier. The child who is born haemophiliac has a painful and brief lifespan ahead. The slightest bruise leads to internal bleeding. These children suffer intensely!

In the best-known family tree, this genetic mutation arose in Queen Victoria of England from whom it spread through the royal families of Europe. The inherited nature of the disease was understood. But the frightening fact for population control is that the carrier-women in the royal families have had as many or more children as noncarriers. The sufferings of their sons and siblings did not deter them. Pressures to breed were too great. This kind of pressure is not confined to royalty. It is alive in our own society. Most children's hospitals in the U.S. are caring for *brothers* who are bleeders. Our penny drives help to sustain their suffering. In 1970 doctors required a thousand pints of human blood to extract enough clotting factor for one operation on one haemophiliac. Death control is in control, nothing voluntary about it.

But there could be! Once we determine to undo our chronic bias toward births and mere existence, death control will come into its own, as a great human accomplishment, a value in line with other values. Social change spreads very rapidly by means of communication. Once the merit is made clear, pressure can shift rapidly toward life control.

This is no longer the era of invading hordes or mass migrations into open space. Today, the most prestigious countries east and west, are those with low birth rates, growing economies and nearly a hundred percent literacy. These are goals which lift the human spirit, which make it possible for the mass of common workmen to share in the enterprise of being human, of belonging beyond town and nation to the exciting world.

The Human Epidemic

11

TIME HAS LOOMED over the human epidemic, disguising it from our perception, until almost too late. We are tuned to medium wavelengths of experience. We notice night and day, the return of seasons, the spells of rain and drought, the growing of children. But the epidemic of births we do not need to notice. The doubling tables, 1600-1850-1930-1972, which tell so much are not felt within our daily grind. Growth was not a personal experience until the last doubling. Now a visible increase of suburbs and loss of farms, increase of smog, the death of Lake Erie have happened in a single lifetime, if that lifetime is fifty years long. Even yet, young reproducers cannot be expected to feel population change within their own lifespan, although they experience its pressures.

It is quite possible, if we are deliberately or hopefully blind, to experience this or that change, this or that symptom, and deny the full, terrible presence of an epidemic.

If the cycle can be interrupted at any point in the interval between birth and new reproduction, then acceleration of the human epidemic will be halted and the prospects of control are good. But we cannot halt epidemics unless we recognize them, and move in on them as soon as possible.

The extent of a classic epidemic depends upon the attack rate: the percentage of those who are susceptible and get the illness. Speed of the epidemic depends upon incubation time after exposure to the disease. Severity of illness depends upon the virulence of the attack. Last, but most important, the size of the epidemic depends upon the total numbers of the susceptible population.

A small group of susceptibles can have a high attack rate and a large group of susceptibles can have a low attack rate, yet the amount of illness may be exactly the same. Likewise a small group of breeders may have a high birth rate and a large group of breeders may have a low birth rate, yet the numbers of births may be exactly the same. Many of the great epidemics of history have occurred with both high attack rate and large populations of susceptible people.

The really frightening epidemics, however, are the ones like plague, where illness almost always means a fatal outcome. The epidemic of pregnancy is frightening because where death control is in control, it means the fateful outcome of a live birth and surviving child. Thus, the present success of our reproduction is a measure of its epidemic deadliness.

The human epidemic is highly contagious. Almost 85% of breeding-age females produce children. This is a very high attack rate, higher than for any plague in history. We are dealing with an almost total susceptibility in this class of human female.

It is natural to think of human incubation time as nine months. But the epidemic of births occurs not in nine-month waves, but in waves of sixteen to twenty-five years. Twenty years is a convenient norm. The speed of the human epidemic depends upon how soon each girl born now produces her first child. The size of the epidemic depends upon how many mothers there are, and how many daughters they produce. We can think of this as an influenza epidemic continuing every year, each year with new susceptibles joining the breeding pool. But unlike influenza, each year guarantees a recurrence on a larger base twenty years later.

A sudden and unusual concentration of susceptibles has preceded many outbreaks of plagues in history. Wars, famines,

floods, and now population increase concentrate humans together in vulnerable masses. Suddenly, because death control is
in control, there is no loss of the first crop of mothers and
daughters. The second crop twenty years later is much larger
than anyone dreamed. No pattern of restraint has intervened.
On a totally susceptible population, with none of its previous
losses, death control prepares the birth epidemic of the third
twenty years. We are not harvesting mothers and children, as
any natural population is harvested. Each cycle is expanding
upon the previous expansion. The effect is frightening. The epidemic potential increases, not only for further human births,
but now again for all the historic ills of plague and virus.

Time is the hidden factor around which our hopes must
swing. We take comfort each year in the fact that the babies
born this year will not produce babies for twenty years more,
which gives us time to work. But this very lag makes the crisis
invisible to the public. It stalls action, makes hurry seem impet-
uous and insistence not very nice.

But hurry is desperate. Those babies of twenty years from
now are on the way. We are in the middle of the second wave
after World War II, preparing the unimaginable impact of the
third wave, those children's children. The sonorous ring, the
sweet patriarchal melody of that phrase, "our children's children", lures us and lulls us to disaster. Unless and until the parents having children today can be brought to feel this epidemic
personally, as an emotion of dread sweeping over their skins, as
knots in the pit of the stomach, as nightmares at midnight,
nothing will be done fast enough, no measure will go far
enough, in fact nothing adequate may be attempted at all. So
long as death control seems kind to us, and life control inhu-
mane, birth will accelerate. The epidemic will run.

We have seen that the blind reaction to save life at any cost
may cost us all life. We cannot look to medicine nor to government, nor to political leadership. Not yet, anyway. A few scientists outside the delivery of medical care, a few biologists, a few

writers—these are the voices outside the compulsory grip of death control who call us to rescue ourselves. Fortunately the young are on the verge of a massive response to them, a mass refusal to take part in the third wave of the epidemic of births.

There has been nothing voluntary about these events. They have happened to us like the events in a Greek drama, as though it were inevitable and not within the power of the intellect or the passion of man to alter. But man is sceptical of his limits. Language, communication, contact of mind with unlike mind is a peculiar feature of our times, its peculiar ecology. If we were to feel suddenly that our lives depended upon matching death control with life control, we would make the change. In the past, people died rather than be converted to new religions, new languages, new foods. But enough of them changed or we would not be here, with the first fateful imprints of man in the dust of the moon. We will be here a long time if suddenly life control not death control governs our impulse to reproduce.

Why Wait Till India?

12

WE CONSTANTLY HEAR that there is no population problem in America; that India and Egypt are serious problems but *we* ought not to cut back *our* growth rate since we are a very productive country and can take care of lots more people. A wider, more personal understanding of what we have done, what we are doing to produce the present impasse between people and resources must come home to the ordinary workman and the owners of the industrial complex. We should have more respect for natural systems in America and for the existing eco-balance in countries around the world. Poverty elsewhere is not irrelevant to the riches of the industrial countries.

Difference in living standards is destined to be a temporary affair. We cannot raise these vast populations to the level of the American consumer, because limits upon resources will very quickly prevent such an effort. We can lose our own standard of living, and that rather quickly, if nations controlling raw materials refuse to export them to us. We can foresee a leveling down and a leveling up between have and have-not nations. A reduction in worldwide population will obviously permit more leveling up. Because of our high consumption per capita, and our deep involvement in technology, we ought to lead the way to fewer people, not claim immunity from this task because we are not poor yet. This would be like congratulating ourselves amid an outbreak of plague because the flea has not yet bitten us!

We have not yet given up hope that the poor can be less poor, the rich less rich in a rational society. However, we can make the rich poor without making the poor at all richer, due to the vast increase in sheer human numbers ahead of us in the next two decades.

India and Egypt are already victims of modern death control. The west offered its new medical skills unwisely and too well after World War II to these areas where high birth rate and high death rate were natural. We looked with compassion and shock on the high infant mortality and set to work in good faith to do something about it as fast as possible. We did and they did. The drastic fall of infant mortality was not offset by a fall in the birth rate. Large families are still the pattern in these countries even twenty-five years later. For the west, drop in family size took place as a slow adaptation to improving conditions over three centuries. We were fortunate, because we had first to discover and then slowly to multiply and deliver the health measures which have made the worldwide revolution in the patterns of births and deaths.

For India, the change began around 1910. At that time, the population of India was slightly over two hundred million which is the population America reached in 1968. During World War I, the population of India grew only slowly thanks to epidemics and battles. However, when peace came the rate of increase picked up speed as health measures improved. Virtual wiping out of smallpox, plague and malaria dropped the death rate steeply. Death rates in the sixties have continued to fall to the very low figure of 18/1000 reported by India in 1969. The birth rate during this period hardly declined at all. In 1910, it was guessed to be close to 40/1000. In 1969, it was still close to 40/1000. In this period, India's total population has risen from two hundred million to more than five hundred million and is still going up rapidly, thirteen million a year.

Such growth has caused concern in scientific and governmental circles for at least twenty years. Yet most Indians, even the educated, hardly recognized this immense creeping disaster.

As India grew from two hundred million she was not aware of population pressure. Instead, she was aware of low productivity, of unemployment, of excessive fragmentation of land. She felt need for electric power, increase in irrigation and food production, and more industrial capacity. Furthermore, the lack of all these was blamed conveniently upon the British. Only in the last decade, with greatly improved census data has the full magnitude of the problem come home to the world. It is not just India's problem. The rest of the world has been supporting India's attempts to modernize now one way, now another. No one is prepared to say how deep a shadow would fall across the human spirit if the subcontinent fails in its bid for stable government and happier people. Conditions for happiness depend upon enough food. Enough food depends upon limitation of births, and both of these depend upon peace between factions. As we shall see again and again in the coming years, the psychic reaction to density makes peace unlikely whenever an essential item like jobs or food is in short supply.

In India, 40% of the population is under fifteen. This 40% of the population will come to childbearing in the next few years at the age usual for India of sixteen, seventeen, eighteen. The children they will produce guarantee that the country will reach a billion before the end of the century unless disaster intervenes. This is the appalling threat promised by the youngsters now crowding the streets of every city, town and village in India. This population exists and will not foreseeably be stopped from breeding. Populations have doubled rapidly before, of course. But this disaster lies in doubling from such an already enormous base. Even to halve the birth rate of 40/1000 would not solve the problem because the death rate has already fallen below 20/1000. It is still falling. The lead time during which births have greatly exceeded deaths is approaching seventy years in India.

Americans know little about this sort of crisis, nor how it

could arise without being noticed. Yet we are a fascinating, a fatal sixty years behind India. We do not notice. We hardly feel population pressure. In 1968, we reached two hundred million, exactly where India was in 1910. We have a relatively low birth rate in our own estimation. But it is double our death rate. Throughout the past decade, our growth rate has been 1.3— lower than India's 2.2 but fast enough to double in sixty years. We also have an extremely young population. If these youngsters follow the birth pattern of their parents we, too, shall double rapidly. We can reach three hundred million before the end of the century.

But *why wait till India?* If they had it to do over again, they would not reach this level of population. Far from it. Today they are energetically advocating two children or less, and undertaking massive government programs in sterilization and contraception. Hindu reservations about abortion are due to fall before the wide spread use of this measure as well.

In 1910, the population of India was already too great for her ancient exhausted soil. They had neither the techniques nor the awareness to halt at two hundred million. Right now, we have both. We can see the problem. We have techniques that will do, although we do not have the leaders. As recently as 1968, Alan Guttmacher of Planned Parenthood–World Population was saying that as long as birth rates continue to drop we have nothing to worry about! All the time rates drop, the total grows rapidly, and rates themselves are expected to bounce back up as the new crop of families from the postwar boom come into production. We cannot help ourselves, we cannot halt growth or deal with the crisis if such is our supposed leadership, such the shortsighted vision. From every side comes the old refrain, from labor, from agriculture, from business, from the pope. We can, we can, we can—produce all the food we need, the jobs we need, the housing we need.

But we don't. We produce food but we fail to get it to many of even our own people. The poor do not select a good diet, even when they can get one. We do not have all the jobs we need. We lead the world in housing but we do not produce all the housing we need, and we are falling steadily further and further behind. We can build all the cities we need and they can be models of modern life. But the fact is that we do not have *even one city* that is a model of modern life. The burden of proof that we can do any of these things while population doubles from its present base falls on those who make the claim. But the burden will crush all of us if they are wrong.

Growth is no more inevitable than misery, than exploitation or poverty. Growth does not hang over us like some edict from God under which we are helpless. Each generation in America has tackled a new set of problems. Behind our political activity is the energetic attitude that we can do something, preferably something simple and easy, about our most pressing problems. Why wait till India before we check ourselves? It is easy to add people. It takes a disaster to get rid of them. And disasters like Biafra and the famines in the Punjab have shocked the confidence of the liberal and the young in our ability to be human. We cannot guarantee our behavior in ever-increasing densities.

Modern life depends upon not having too many people for the political, educational and medical systems. We are watching these systems disintegrate under pressure. Food must come in, waste must go out of our cities. Water supply must be continuous. Disease must be contained. There is a definite upper limit for all kinds of human associations beyond which they are ineffective in carrying out their original purpose. Effort is dissipated in friction. Yet none of our thinking has centered upon what the desirable upper limits of a people might be. If politicians and planners have ever asked what is the upper limit of population they have done so only to bypass, to circumvent it. Greed leads our planning for more people, because greed has identified more people with more purchasers. Unfortunately, promoters really accept this idea. Consequently in the sixties, galloping growth, rampant speculation and riotous living carted us away on a wave of TV commercials about the good life.

Doubling our population is not inevitable. But it will happen to us unless our patterns of births and deaths change right now, unless zero growth becomes the target and we zero in on it with all the means we have and can develop. It is incredible that we have made such a distinction between this health measure and all other health measures. The future ecological needs of man require that we turn our habits of thought upsidedown. We should not ask how to increase the critical mass, how to plan for twice our people. We need to ask how to design our cities and our families so that we can live below our present population.

One look at India, one look at ourselves, warns us that we have been misled. It is obvious that good adjectives have become attached to bad facts; that our attitudes toward growth in America are not impartial but manipulated. Just as ghettoes and genocide misrepresent our cities and our programs, so "glorious growth" misrepresents the facts of population.

Sex

13

THROUGHOUT human history, islands, mountain ranges and marriage circles have isolated human groups from one another. Whenever a group is relatively isolated over a long period of time, selection fosters its divergence from the rest. Groups distrust each other because they are different, and they now will not stop breeding because they want more of their own kind. On the other hand, whenever free gene exchange occurs over a wide area, selection favors a more homogenous people. Our population history reflects repeated isolatings, differings and comings together again in gene exchange, which is population language for sexual acts producing offspring. There would have been no selection, no gene exchange and no population explosion without sexual difference and sexual intercourse.

The sexual drive is a basic part of the population problem in every country. Men and women learn their sexual attitudes from the social group into which they have been born, and only explicit later education can modify this early training, or reveal to the individual that he has been actually trained. We allow rough-housing and tickling to go on. Then suddenly, we interfere. We pull down the skirts of little girls and take little boys' hands from their trousers. Without knowing why, the child has come upon a borderline which is etched in his memory forever. The mixture of shame and innocence, and alerted curiosity will be carried forward into all the sexual advances and retreats of growing up. The areas and actions which carry this intense emotional color from childhood can rarely become neutral for the adult.

Some societies cause harmony and pleasure between the sexes; some cause fear and taboo; some specialize in antagonisms. Sexual behavior depends upon genetics, upon inherited hormone levels and sexual potency, but the major differences in behavior between peoples are not genetic. They result from cultural patterns which dictate when and how sexual intercourse may occur between a man and a woman, and what sort of provision must be made for rearing the child. Social control of sexual relations often conflicts with personal desire for them. All of this is included in the new term, sexuality.

What lies behind the sudden interest in sexuality and the demand for sex education? While public education finances many unimportant subjects, sex involves all of us in more ways than any other topic now mentioned in school. So the idea that education should include sexuality merits a tolerant attitude. Comparison of sexual codes, examination of sexual behavior, the proposing of sexual responsibility does not threaten the young in our society; it threatens the sexually inhibited, the sexually deprived, the sexually middle-aged. It also threatens certain reticences and idealizations which spring afresh in the human heart and which ought not to be disregarded. It is wise to remember how many happy couples, yearning lovers and loved children have lived in the world knowing nothing whatever about the facts of life, the existence of fertilization, or the 501 positions of intercourse. Knowledge has not been a precondition of sexual pleasure or sexual responsibility in the past. Why then do we need it? Why not leave it in the universities and medical schools where so many guardians of the public morals are eager to return it?

There is evidence that disapproval of sexual pleasure in or out of marriage becomes destructive of that pleasure. Ignorance of differing codes of sexual behavior causes either sexual experimentation or rejection of sexual adventure altogether. Better sexual, and therefore better marital, adjustments are the stated hope of many educators.

The most intelligent rationale for sex education was given by Margaret Mead. Each culture and each subculture has its own sexual customs, grown up over time. Modern complex societies cross many cultural lines. This exposure to other subcultures is multiplied by our large public schools, especially as young people move up the educational track from junior high into high school and college. They meet a wider cross section of students their own age than any previous generation. They meet them away from home patterns and control of behavior. They do not know how to interpret each other's signals, sexual and otherwise. The extreme age-grading fostered by the American school system deprives youngsters of someone a little older and more experienced to ask. Hence a general level of information upon the reproduction process protects all youngsters.

Knowledge of dating and mating behavior is thought desirable, prior to the occasion when such knowledge will be needed. Sex education prior to puberty has more value and less emotional overtones than later. Precocious children need to know about sex. They also need to respect the fact that others are innocent. The innocent need to know that not everybody considers this a state of bliss. Possibly both objectives might have been reached without disturbing public moralities with "sexuality" and "sex education." It has hardly been helpful to start the public looking for its sexuality as though it were a breast or a penis it had somehow failed to discover.

The protectors of morality have hardly helped either. Calling pornography a communist plot is clever nonsense. Confusing communism and pornography with the desire for information on sex is, however, deliberate falsehood. Giving and receiving sex information is a natural human desire in all cultures. However disguised, sex education and sexuality are here to stay. In the space age, we can hardly send our children back to the cabbage patch or the stork. They are demanding more and more of the truth, and working out their own decisions about it.

Understanding sex as a part of our natural history, and considering its social effects in human life is necessary if we are to develop methods of preventing pregnancy. Also, we can better judge the claim that the proper route to fewer births is fewer sexual relations. Sex itself is a mystery, one of the most elusive events in the evolution of life. The dark field of the microscope reveals an amoeba to be a sugary-looking little creature, irregular and changeable as a cumulus cloud on a summer day. It is without skeleton or apparent structure of any kind. Yet the creature moves now in one direction, now in another by a process of flowing, and it will pull back from an irritating needle or salt crystal as rapidly as it will flow around something pleasing. Contained in an invisible surface which holds it together like a drop of oil in water, it has the same kind of quick yes-or-no response as we ourselves do. In a plentiful food supply this animal grows to a tiny limit controlled by its surface-to-volume ratio, and then it divides into two smaller animals. In the infinitely many generations of amoebae, something refuses to die. Controlling growth, activity and heredity, it continues to divide, century after century.

Individual amoebae will sometimes be attracted to each other. A bridge of cellular material will form and the contents of these two living drops will flow into each other. For a time the population of such rejuvenated amoebae grows more vigorously, feeds more actively and shows quicker responses to stimuli.

In this primitive form of exchange of cell material, we have a tentative model for all later forms of sexuality. Everyone knows the human baby grows more vigorously, shouts and cries and kicks with more energy than his parents. He is rejuvenated all right! However, between the human infant and the rejuvenated amoeba, lies a long and fascinating development of sexual patterns.

The most startling change from the amoeba is the occurrence of the egg. Only after some arrangement, however primitive, had been made for the escape and survival of germ cells could adults afford to die. Death and the egg arrived together on the living scene and life cannot now continue without them.

Cell materials designed to carry forward the life of the species can be better protected if they are not directly involved in the wear and repair of the individual's daily life. When the germ plasm of animals became set aside for egg and sperm production, the body cells of animals could be devoted to a more energetic and risky individual life.

One of the primary obligations laid upon the rising chain of plants and animals was the production of special cells from which new life could spring. The male pollen and the male sperm are fascinatingly parallel. The male pollen becomes motile and sends out a tube many times its length into the female flower. Down this tube the male cell nucleus and hereditary sap now flow to reach the female cell and combine to form the seed. The parent plant may live many years and bear many seed crops like a tree; or it may die as some summer flowers do, after only one season. The story of plant evolution and dispersion is the story of many techniques developed for scattering pollen to the female flowers, for protecting the fertilized ovary of the flower, and for surrounding it with protective seed coats, husks or shells. The beautiful and delicate parachutes of the dandelion and the milkweed seeds insure far dispersal in air, just as the buoyant husk of the coconut floats it from island to island.

The evolution of animals took a different tack. The shedding of eggs and sperm into the water gradually became a precisely timed spawning favoring fertilization. Salmon return to the riv-

ers of their origin, heavy with eggs and milt, and fat from feasting in the sea. The long journey up through fresh water is
made without feeding. The female swims upstream, digs out a
clean gravel redd, and spawns her eggs in the gravel. At the
same time a male darts into the pool and sheds his milt in the
water of the redd. The billions of sperm release in a white
cloud. Thousands surround each egg, though only one sperm
makes entry and fertilizes the cell. The fertilized egg, through
autumn drought, winter cold and spring flood has only the
gravel to protect it. In spring, the little fish may hatch and escape to sea. But millions never make it. Each step of the way
they contribute to the food chain of other animals.

The next development was the protection of the egg during
hatching. All kinds of attached or guarded eggs and larvae now
exist. Crabs carry their fertilized eggs outside the body, but attached under the protective tail segments. Crayfish and lob-
sters carry first the eggs, then the tiny hatched babies as well.
The octopus hangs her eggs on the underside of rocks and defends them vigorously. Unlike dispersal of fertilized seeds,
increased protection of the egg became the animal pattern.

Thus with internal fertilization, internal growth of the embryo became possible. Internal growth permits a considerable
reduction in the number of eggs. An energy-budget devoted to
producing fewer eggs can maintain them in the female body to
advanced stages of development.

The marine rosefish grows to be twelve or fifteen years old,
and produces a maximum of live-born young when not less
than ten. Little rosefish are perfectly formed inside the translu-
cent egg coat and are shed into the ocean by the hundreds as
tiny swimming fish during the plankton-rich months of spring
and summer.

The familiar guppy has fewer and larger young at one time,
but the idea—protection for the young fish until they can hide
and feed—is similar. The rosefish until it became popular as
ocean-fresh fillets in the frozen market, was successful and

abundant. Fishing for the adults has dropped the average age of the stock into the earliest of its reproductive years. This is a seriously threatened fishery. At present, no protection can be given the breeding stock because it is fished by trawls which crush male and female, young and old alike. Internal development of the embryo and live birth of young gave the rosefish an advantage in the sea because its infancy was protected. But because an older, more richly developed maternal system is delicious to eat, man, the predator, is fast undoing this previous advantage.

The egg of land animals required protection from drying first of all. All egg-laying land animals either lay in the water or provide a water-conserving shell. Salamanders and frogs have a water-living tadpole stage. Snakes and birds developed membranes and shell to protect the fertile egg and the young embryo. Only in truly aquatic animals does external fertilization still take place. Mammals, birds, reptiles and insects must copulate or mate, and the male must place the sperm inside the female so that moist female tissues can protect them.

Development of the fertilized egg inside the female could not take place without internal fertilization. Like the male pollen tube of plants, animals also developed male devices for the internal fertilization of eggs. Some lower animals make sperm packets which the female attaches to herself until the eggs are ready to shed. Other males have structures like the guppy's modified fin which can inject the sperm directly into the female. But in many marine animals and in land animals, a true penis developed to insert sperm into the female opening.

Timing of fertilization became more and more important. Cyclicity developed. Breeding seasons, heat and oestrus followed. The trend in land animals continued toward longer development inside the mother after fertilization, and toward fewer young born at any one time. Rather than waste adults in breeding only once, adulthood became extended. Birth itself became a process far more complex than the shedding of ripened eggs into the sea. The animals we know best are animals with a long interval between fertilization and birth. For many months after birth the mother gives milk to nourish the young. Humans and elephants endure the longest gestation, lactation and dependence of young, of all the animals.

The female deer or cattle come into heat like the familiar carnivores, and the rodents. In these periods of womb preparation and egg production, females will accept a male and stand for him while he mounts them, inserts the penis, and pumps into them the combination of sperm and protective fluids called semen. In these groups of animals, the male will mount any female in heat if he can, and will serve any female that will stand for him. He will not be interested in any female not in heat, and he will not be able to serve or impregnate any female that will not stand for him. The whole process takes only a few minutes, and is repeated several times perhaps during the term of a day or so. Then the female goes out of heat, and is presumably bred. If she is not, another heat period will return in a few weeks. Meanwhile they lose interest in each other. The male looks elsewhere.

Humans are peculiar among mammals in having no heat period. The male can mount any female any time if she accepts him. Depending upon mood and preference, but not related to the condition of egg or womb, the female may accept him repeatedly. Women are fertile around the year, and children can be born in any month.

Something extremely important and aberrant happened to us in the long past which separated us from all those animals in whom sex occurs in cycles and for whom asexual periods return throughout their reproductive lives. In the human case, sexual interest persists into pregnancy and returns during lactation.

This situation has created definite behavior patterns and problems for the human race which do not exist for our most familiar animal friends. We are like all other sexual species in that sex gives us the basis for genetic variation and the possibility of rapid evolution. We are truly isolated, truly unlike all other animals in sexual behavior. One looks without success among animals for that delight in sexual activity itself which so distinguishes the human in the art and literature of every country.

The breeding season of other temperate zone animals relates to the change of light and temperature, and usually insures that the young calf or deer will be dropped in the months of spring or early summer pasture. Long ago, before the end of the last glaciation, human tribes were spread all over Asia and Europe, and they knew the use of fire. If men came from a tropical center and developed fire before they spread to colder climates, there would be no special time of year for them, like the calving and fawning times of grazing animals. The young would be favored not by the slow progression of sun and stars, but by the rude bonfires and the rough skins and the crude cherishing of a human society. The hallmark of our difference is expressed by our *indifference* to time of year in breeding and in birth.

But even this does not explain to us the daily eagerness, the daily undercurrent of sexual invitation. It surely is not necessary to production of young. Like the cow and the deer, we have only one child a year or at most a twinning, and for this a very short season would suffice. The oestrus system produces ample herds and would produce ample humans.

Continuous sexual readiness is not necessary for reproductive success, so far as we can judge. Even in primitive conditions human sexual relations do not always lead to childbirth. In modern societies it is the exception rather than the rule for coitus to lead to pregnancy. This is true even where no methods whatever are used for prevention. Coitus is sought and enjoyed for its own sake, hundreds of times a year quite apart from the few days each month when it might prove fertile. But if this is so, some advantage must accrue to the group, to the family unit, or to the young from sexual pleasure apart from reproduction.

Sexual pleasure is supposed to strengthen the pair bond necessary for raising children. But this is dubious. Until recently few societies have considered the physical desires of the couple to be important. Kinship, or material wealth mattered much more. The middle-class girl is inhibited by subtle yet completely effective disapprovals from touch and grooming with young men until a suitor is approved. Then the young couple can do their best to overcome the well-taught blocks to sexual companionship and enjoyment. The young girl will become pregnant whether she enjoys her husband or not. The natural affection for children is reinforced by strong social pressure to do well by them. Until Freud, this was regarded by most societies as sufficient to enforce the pair bond. Sexual pleasure and marriage might overlap but hardly require each other.

Sexual pleasure may help to hold an unrelated group of breeding-age males within the social unit. Except when engaged in a common task, the young male has equivocal reactions to other males. The possibility of common enterprise is fostered by vying for a female. In studies of the higher apes, the dominant males preoccupied by females with infants are materially buffered by the large, fluctuant group of young adults who can be roused in emergencies. In rural human societies such bachelor groups are found following the harvest, putting up barns, breaking horses and turning out for emergencies of fire and flood. Erotic interest develops among the group, especially if the young girls share in these activities by providing food and admiration. Thus actual and prospective sexual pleasure becomes an advantage to the whole society. Larger units may hold together than would occur in seasonal societies with a strict breeding season. The same possibility of erotic adventure and exchange pervades the modern campus, and surely is an unspoken but potent force in keeping hundreds of non-intellectual youngsters in this way-station between home and life. Enticement pervades the mixed office and the factory line. Group cohesion may be the most important secondary function in human society of the unusual sexual readiness of man.

One thing is perfectly clear; we shall have to deal with the fact that coitus occurs far in excess of reproduction, that it has done so throughout human history, and therefore throughout a long prehistory. Due to pressures of population, couples will no doubt have fewer children spontaneously, and soon, but hardly because of fewer sexual relations. In the past it was possible to ignore, to suppress, to regiment the sexual drives of the young in strict societies. In the wave of present educational and social changes, we cannot expect the young of the next decades to settle for these repressions of the past. The reality of erotic desire, of emotional depth, of this human comforting will not fit into a one-to-one relationship with family formation, especially if family formation itself comes later, is more valuable and briefer in duration. There is no use being twice-minded about it. Sexual patterns and controls are one problem and birth patterns and controls are another. We will not come to creative solutions and realistic understanding of either problem so long as we mix them with confused moralities.

Sexual pleasure is many things to many people. For some it is a target for regulation and interference in other lives. For others, it is the constructive and creative dimension in human relations. No pleasure is easily measured and reduced to science. For this reason, our scientific century has documented sexual illness, rather than sexual health, has looked at despairs and crimes rather than joys and creations. Yet every culture has its love stories and its god-like lovers. Every culture means by this something more than mere mating. Vistas of peace, moments of unearthly trust and relaxation which the day and the task forbid; yearnings for beauty dimly grasped are universal forces in the social development of humans, in the amelioration of savagery. Only slowly are the disciplines of anthropology, psychiatry and medicine converging upon common notions of sexual health. Only slowly are they admitting the value of the artists' amorous joy. We do not need perfect or Utopian understanding. Acceptance of the need for tolerance and inquiry is enough. Set forth in simple terms and made available early in life, these notions of joy and of sexual health can be expected to have a profound effect upon human happiness.

We are not equations to be reduced to the common terms of an animal past, but expansions of those terms, ancestors of the unexpected. The brain convoluted by the effort to jump accurately across high trees has evolved the computer. The eye perfected to gauge hunting distance has devised those circumventors of distance, the telescope and the microscope. The sexual drive to produce offspring overflows into all the sensuous arrays of art. There is no question but that the sexual energies of humans are so great and so creative they can overflow into a transformation of personal life. Let loose from mindless reproduction, pointed toward sharing, toward joy, who knows what the sexual drive can lead to in the future of the species?

Genes and Genocide

14

In many communities, misunderstanding of sexuality caused sex education to be opposed at first. Similarly, misunderstanding of genocide caused some opposition to the first efforts in population education.

First of all, no one has ever seen a gene. In the last century, the masters of cellular discovery and microscopic technique laid the groundwork for the modern gene theory. Ever since, the nucleus of the living cell has been assumed to contain the physical material of heredity. The gene was a useful construct; an idea invented, like the atom and its electrons, to satisfy certain puzzling, observed events. In heredity, the gene has been assigned two roles: to control the shape and function of living tissues in an individual, and to pass on these shapes and functions from one generation to another. Thus, individuals and populations have special genetic characteristics which reflect their history and produce their individuality.

Genocide is a more recent word constructed upon the same root. It refers not to the killing of a gene but to the deliberate wiping out of a people so that they leave no descendants. The wiping out of a people could occur by outright murder and pogrom, or by castration. Fear of these events is deep; longing for immortality for one's own kind is natural. So genocide has become an infamous word since the concentration camps of Nazi Germany gave rise to it in World War II. Now it is being used among racial, religious and linguistic minorities around the globe. In America, genocide has been hurled as an epithet into the controversies over birth control and abortion. This has caused some to back away from birth control, while others have been tempted to use genocide as a rallying cry. Therefore the issue must be understood and the challenge met, in order for population programs to receive funding and support.

Genocide is a truly rare event in human history. In the past, populations tended to survive in their genetic uniqueness, despite invasion, intermarriage and conquest. Even after a thousand years of being confined together on relatively small islands, the Irish, Welsh, Scots and Britons remain distinct populations with differing political objectives. Through the centuries, they killed each other with vigor, intermarried and raised each other's orphans, but genocide was not the outcome.

In modern times, deliberate attempts at genocide produced one of the most terrible decimations of history, the Jewish exodus from Europe. Yet even this population has not been wiped out.

Real genocide came to some of the Amerinds, however. The tribes truly suffered and fought and died and lost heart as many conquered peoples have done in human history. Foreign diseases completed the loss. Today, some of the smaller tribes number only a few hundred. If they are to survive as ethnic units, they need to bear fewer children and raise more of them to maturity in what is left of their valuable traditions. On the other hand, the larger Indian tribes are merely compounding their problems by having large families and neglecting birth control.

From this perspective, when a large minority of more than thirty million Negro citizens are urged to protest against genocide in family planning programs, something is being misrepresented. It is absurd to suppose that genocide could result from offering this population a pill to take, a condom to use, or a device that can be removed. Only ignorant people or leaders deliberately trying to mislead the ignorant can possibly confuse the two.

Probably behind this misuse of genocide lies the bitter belief that unless the minority becomes a majority they cannot succeed as a people, they cannot expect justice or get ahead. The original government of America was designed to protect minorities and to secure their rights against the majority. Thus, wherever the cry of genocide is successful in opposing birth control, there some minority feels unprotected and deprived of justice. There some majority has failed to carry out representative government. But then family planning is the wrong target to blame!

While the loose talk of genocide was designed to stir up feelings, the demographic facts tell a different story. The Negro has always outbred the white groups he lived among, yet this did not guarantee him success. The high Negro birth-rate, one and one-half times that of whites, contributed to their low position in the labor scale. Jewish communities have been more shrewd. They also met bitter prejudice. They had small families and concentrated upon educating them. The consequence has been professional success, rising affluence and influence for the Jewish community. Furthermore, with the lowering of religious walls, the sexual walls have been coming down. The American Jewish community is merging by intermarriage and dispersion from its original centers.

When the word genocide crops up in opposition to family planning, what other fears and misconceptions are being hinted at, and what can be done about them?

Fears of genocide may arise from real ignorance of the difference between castration and contraception. Castration makes it impossible for the male to produce sperm cells. While it usually refers to cutting out the male testicles, castration can be accomplished in other ways. Sperm are the main product of the testis. However the male hormones which control sperm production are also made there. These hormones produce the male look—beard, body hair and deep voice—and also produce the male sex drive. In castration the hormone-producing cells are removed as well as the sperm-producing cells, and the male loses his sexual character, including ability to erect the penis or respond physically to sexual stimulation. This is considered a shattering loss by most males. If real or imagined castration has been used as a punishment for "sex crimes" and such crimes have a racial overtone, the passions stirred up are not easily returned to levels of reason and fact.

Contraception, or the prevention of pregnancy, is not at all the same as the castration of the male. Castration is performed all the time to produce hogs, wethers, steers, capons and geldings as a part of rural life. The more complex procedures of contraception and sterilization are quite different. It is most important to make this distinction. Leaders of men ought to make themselves clear on these subjects, and be responsible for talking about them correctly to other men and boys.

Due to mass sterilizations in World War II, sterilization is also a source of confusion and fear. Nevertheless, whenever prevention of births is essential, whether for health or for social reasons, sterilization is best. Sterilization as it is performed today on the male does *not* interfere with the hormone cells of the testis; the male hormones are fed into the blood stream undisturbed and maintain the sexual character, the response to sexual stimulation and the ability to erect and ejaculate. Males who understand that it does not affect those qualities considered "manly" are satisfied with the operation and enjoy a better sexual life than before. There is nothing "manly" about producing unwanted children. Vasectomy removes this fear.

Thus genocide is not an accurate charge against contraceptive programs, and those who understand the differences between contraception, vasectomy and castration are unlikely to make it.

The one excuse for interjecting this term into population discussion lies in the recent history of poverty cities in America. Birth-control clinics in the recent past were placed where poor women live because improved medical care of the poverty mother begins with limiting births. No other measure brings so much physical relief to her or her family at so moderate a cost. Birth itself is a high risk for the poverty mother. Infant mortality wastes her nine months of pregnancy at a higher rate than for other women. Thus the energy-budget of the family cannot be set in balance until she can manage to escape the dreary round of pregnancy and birth.

Birth control is a medical service easily obtained from private doctors. The woman who is aggressive can go to a clinic. But the least motivated, least energetic, most needy mothers do not do so. The clinic has to go to her. The poorer she is, the more children she has, the less likely she is to spend the time away from home, or the carfare, if she can get it, to venture out of her narrow range to find a birth-control clinic. Birth-control clinics are placed where they now are in a direct effort to equalize opportunity by serving the poor. Negro mothers have the same reasons for wanting to limit their families as other women have, only perhaps more so. They know personally that mothers too beaten down by childbearing handicap their children in the battle of life, and they are bitter about the humiliations they receive in attempting to get sterilizations and abortions from the health bureaucracy.

However, the black militants reacted to the location of Planned Parenthood clinics and took up the cry of genocide. It is well to remember that family size is not genetic in humans; it is learned behavior and can be influenced by propaganda. Maturer women have not been influenced. They understand the toll of pregnancy too well. But there has been a rise in out-of-wedlock pregnancy among young blacks. Today, most young women want freedom to get a job or finish college or get food and clothing for the children already born. Wherever there is hope for a better share of goods, women respond positively to birth control and smaller families. Only where there is no hope, no possibility of improvement, is birth control greeted with suspicion and apathy.

Much of the antagonism in health care was triggered by the failure of common courtesy in health departments and clinics offering contraceptive services to the poor. Throughout our great health bureaucracy, hierarchy is deeply imbedded. The poor welfare patient in the past has been treated to a shocking lack of respect. White or black, the citizen on welfare is still a second-class citizen, the target of petty snobs and insecure bureaucrats.

The National Medical Association, an organization of Negro physicians, has led the battle for better medical care for poverty families; it approves birth control for the Negro family as a basic part of health care. This wrangle will settle down to good sense, especially as we move out against the white birth rate.

Generally, it is a mistake to single out the poor for population control even though they stand to benefit from it most. The facts point to a small family for everyone, for the upper and the middle class, for the rural poor and the city poor. One terrible fact is quite clear: there are too many of us already. We are condemning each other to produce more of us for the next little while. This is the road to real genocide.

Unchecked population does in fact mean that the poor of the ghetto will suffer first and physically; not the military, not the political leaders, not the mobile upper classes. Everyone suffers in famine and disorder, but the poor die. Only a stationary population will rebalance itself; only stable people can control their fertility. Whether we like it or not, ritualized conflict and population control lie ahead of us all, if any of us are to survive.

We need an overt population target for everyone in America and America as a whole; then no one sector can be singled out for neglect or genocide or special treatment.

However, until we understand the population dynamics of our cities, the inflow of rural poor at the bottom, the stagnation in unskilled jobs, and the outflow of more successful people at the top, we will not begin to remedy the slum.

Economists like to measure the advancement of a nation by its steep decline in agricultural employment. But they have not taken an equally close look at the decline in human happiness. It is easier to ignore the links between high fertility of rural families, loss of rural employment, and pressure on the slums. In worldwide perspective, the dynamics of the city are similar everywhere. In the last thirty years there has been a rapid increase of chaul, barrio, ghetto, slum. Infant survival has risen as opportunities fall. Political refugees add to the problem. They crowd into cities like Calcutta, Singapore, Hong Kong, New Delhi and New York. Demographers describe these conditions as artificial and temporary, only they are not specific about how artificial, how temporary.

We cannot solve such problems by refusing to look at them. Everywhere birth rates must fall, in-migration must cease and creation of new resources must receive priority. In America, if it so happens that black birth rates, black in-migration and black resources are involved, we cannot rearrange the facts. Instead, we must recognize with honesty where the hardship has been placed. Liberal Americans are full of an inverse racism, which denies the possibility of any differences among us and belabors equality, while overlooking the great strain living up to such notions can impose upon individuals.

Young men and women are warned about cultural shock when they enter the Peace Corps or the Foreign Service, but most of us overlook the cultural shock caused by internal migration to thousands of American families. Somehow we expect that a little job-training and reorientation can alter the responses of a lifetime. Especially the young men are expected to make the middle-class move in their own persons in a matter of months, whereas most middle-class Americans have had at least a generation in which to do so. Also, we have to remember when we talk in global terms of getting rid of the ghetto, that the modern ghetto has attracted and protected the families who have moved to them.

Moving out of poverty implies a moving up in economic scale, but regular employment is very different from unstructured street life, and both are different from the rhythms of the farm. Any 9-to-5 job will present a serious emotional change involving food habits and patterns of sleep and sexual activity. In many cities of the world, stress is compounded by language difference, by fierce pride and quick suspicion. Thus, many men who are able to move into the city are unable to make the second set of adjustments and move out.

Racists give racist reasons for these situations; economists give economic reasons; politicians give political reasons. History records that a citizenry which cannot be fed cannot be governed, and now the ecologist points out that overpopulation is temporary, vulnerable to harvest, wherever it is.

Now we can begin to understand why birth control programs which concentrate on the city poor have not gone to the root of the trouble. Even though large numbers of needy women can be served at low cost in central clinics, even though private patients presumably should look after themselves, it took oversensitive blacks to point out to undersensitive whites that there was something wrong with such a program. Reducing population is a task for everyone. All of us must help to re-establish a balance between people and resources. In view of the crisis coming upon us, the real bigot today is one who believes that more of his own kind are necessary or excusable.

Soberly, then, we should review the arithmetic of birth control programs. In America, large families make up a small part of the population but they make up a large part of the poor. If birth-control programs are to help the poverty child and the poverty mother, then certainly these large families should be the target. Anywhere in the world, prevention of the seventh child directly helps the other six.

Exponential population growth occurs with the third child, however. If birth control programs are to check overall population growth, it is more efficient to concentrate upon third births in the middle-class family. [fig. 3] These are the families that Planned Parenthood has been neglecting. In view of our history and diversity, it is perfectly natural for many people to feel prejudice about birth-control programs. [fig. 4] But once we have paused before these truths and questioned our own bias, then we can resolve not to act out these prejudices any longer. [fig. 5]

The greatest hope for all is that the young will not turn away from education, from difficult special training. In their impatience, the tedium of orderly change bears heavily on the young. The danger is that the intelligent militant will deprive himself of his institutions, and his institutions will be deprived of him.

At some point in the scuffle, the leaders who are demanding opportunity for the Negro will also quietly insist that he measure up. He will cease to hide behind race and race feelings and begin the hard work of using his ability. It is no kindness in the long run; it is inverse snobbery and discrimination to make special exceptions and to lower standards. In the long run it will be better for all to meet one high standard, to join in one society and one higher education. It is not to be expected that all Negro leaders can take the long view. In the first stage of African kinship and identity-seeking, strange exaggerations are bound to appear and disappear. The fact remains that the American Negro drives a car, handles complex money, expects complex benefits and threatens a complex disruption to an advanced if imperfect society. He does not go barefoot, drive bullocks or wrestle subsistence from the farms and fisheries of undeveloped Africa. Between the American Negro and the emerging peoples are differences which are not erased by com-

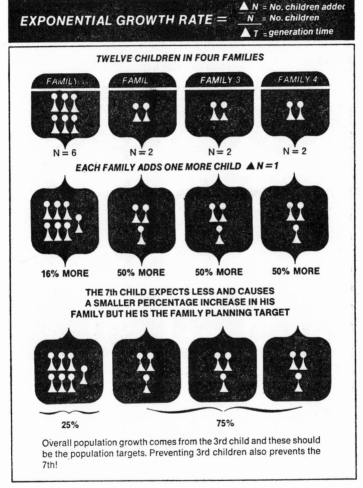

fig. 3

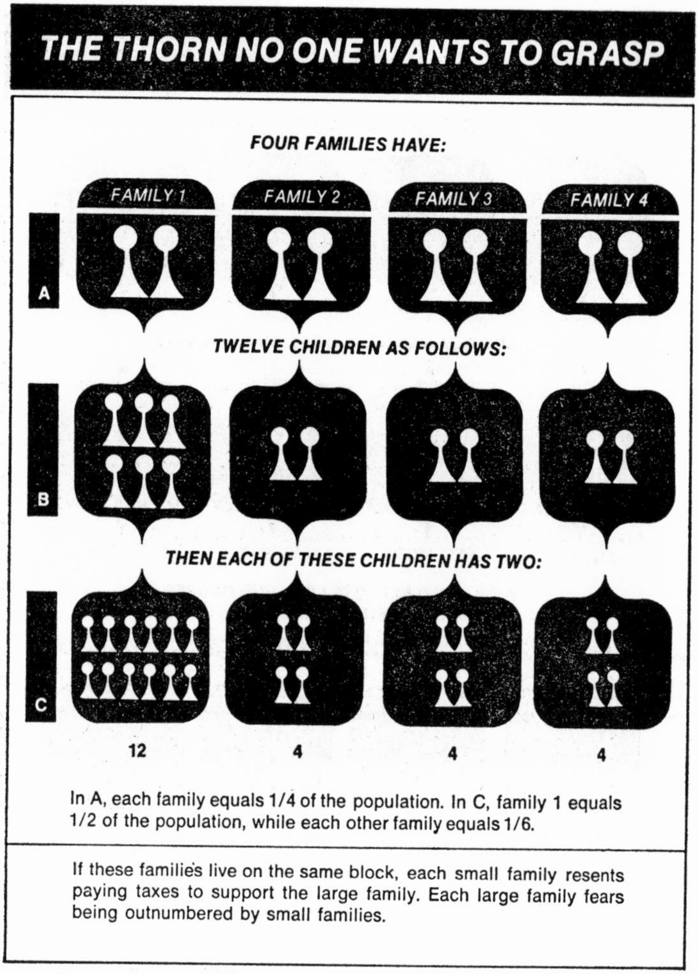

THE THORN NO ONE WANTS TO GRASP

FOUR FAMILIES HAVE:

FAMILY 1　　FAMILY 2　　FAMILY 3　　FAMILY 4

A

TWELVE CHILDREN AS FOLLOWS:

B

THEN EACH OF THESE CHILDREN HAS TWO:

C

12　　　　4　　　　4　　　　4

In A, each family equals 1/4 of the population. In C, family 1 equals 1/2 of the population, while each other family equals 1/6.

If these families live on the same block, each small family resents paying taxes to support the large family. Each large family fears being outnumbered by small families.

fig. 4

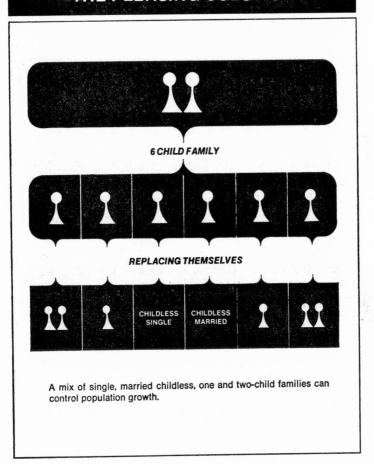

THE PLEASING SOLUTION

6 CHILD FAMILY

REPLACING THEMSELVES

CHILDLESS SINGLE

CHILDLESS MARRIED

A mix of single, married childless, one and two-child families can control population growth.

fig. 5

mon ancestry. The tasks of a common future the American Negro and the African tribes can never expect to share. But the white boy and the black boy in America will live on the same street, and share the future, only if the adults of today believe in sharing. Young people are already moving this way.

The sense of justice, the strong affection of many whites for Negroes are on the side of quick improvement. Currents of better feeling run deep. The white community is tough enough to stand a little excess, while the scales rebalance. Day-to-day improvement is not being written in hot temper nor hot blood, but in white and black faces learning to look quite steadily at each other as they meet.

Unless we can assuage ethnic rivalries we cannot expect to reverse long-term population growth. We have had justifiable, action-producing violence. But violence is basically self-defeating. The social advantages sought by and due to the black community depend upon normal pursuits. It will be sad if we abandon these possibilities on the eve of their coming to be. The best service the white community can do for the black community now is to stand firmly against intimidation, against reply, against emotive charges, and to draw upon deep supplies of humor and patience.

In all animal communities where outright conflict is to be avoided, ritual behavior intervenes. The wolves sniff a boundary line, the jays ruffle and call, the cock pheasant makes the morning ring with his cries, and from the next field another answers him. Provocation and insult beget retaliation. In the present confrontation a ritualized manner, a formality during boundary dispute, is due to replace provocation as a human technique, simply because it is more productive.

American democracy is not legal or economic. It is personal, direct, antipolitical, easy to lapse from, hard to defend. Nevertheless, it is both wise and true to the innermost values of diverse human beings. It singles out equality among the difference and smiles upon it. We don't believe that everyone is created equal. We believe that we should act as though they were. We do not believe everyone is good or honest. But we have to assume that they are, hundreds of times a day. We no longer believe that universal education, and freedom of speech and the press can guarantee us freedom. But we know that without them we are guaranteed to have *no* freedom. We don't think our country is perfect, our laws just, nor our economy fair. But glancing at the international scene, we see ours alive with possibility. The young are a truly political generation thronging on the sidelines, ready to put wrenches in the machinery, to check the steamroller, to divert the flow of money to more human ends.

The world is my country, to serve mankind is my religion.
—Tom Paine

For mankind to serve itself, or for the world to be again every man's country, words like genocide must cease to impede population control.

Madness in Methods

15

In the early years, when to have respite from birth at all was a relief and a novelty, methods of family planning failed at about the same rate and had about the same kind of nuisance value. All of them interfered with spontaneous sex to about the same degree. But the generation breaking trails in contraception was just about to break trails in sexual practice also. Pleasure for women as well as men became the concern of psychiatrists, marriage counselors and social reformers.

Messy methods, ineffective methods common in the thirties are still with us. Today they are clearly unsuited to the job of preventing births. But in their own day they were quite remarkable aids in limiting births for individual couples. This shift in opinion is very obvious in the medical profession. Doctors who graduated before 1940 recall when their young women and their best friends found the condom and the diaphragm not only good enough but also quite daring and progressive. These same gentlemen are now at the top of the obstetrical profession all over the world. They find it hard to admit that these same methods are backward or inhibiting to pleasure, when their own youthful experience ran to the contrary. It comes as a shock to white-haired chiefs of obstetrical services when a young patient ventures to object to the diaphragm because it "freezes her up". Yet remarks like that are deeply meant, in the most serious kind of human protest. A doctor should listen objectively if he can when a woman is courageous enough to honor him with such protest. So, madly, absurdly in good faith and old-fashioned authority, the diaphragm survives in the most expensive private practices, and also in the charity clinics run by these practitioners.

Perhaps the role of the medical profession in modern birth control is not well understood even by those close to it. In America, the obstetrical specialist has made a peculiar pact, a monopoly in restraint of trade! For the exclusive territory of the female organs, and the birth process, he has foresworn all practice on the male. Not even an aspirin! This accounts for some of the clammy receptions that husbands and fathers occasionally still receive around obstetrical offices. It may even be why condoms are sold without prescription! Obstetrics has been the wealthiest of all specialties for the last fifty years. No small factor is the milieu, the delivery room of the local hospital, where the newest and best equipment is provided to doctors without cost. Equipment is paid for by hospital and taxpayer, and recouped from the patient in charges. None of it is paid for by the doctor using it for his own income-producing activity. Furthermore, most hospitals are a private club for doctors admitted to staff privilege, so that only a handful of men can actually use this costly setup. Obstetricians charge consistently high fees, whether they attend the actual birth or not. They may do excellent work. They claim to have dropped maternal deaths and adopted new ways to rescue the newborn, taking to themselves credit for much basic research done by other specialists.

Today, for most women in America, birth is an ugly, streamlined, heartless affair even when the mother is safe and the baby well cared for after delivery. Only the fortunate have any family with them, or are allowed to hold their babies in anything like a normal human relation. Yet as any shepherd knows, a ewe that owns her first lamb right off gets a good milk supply and raises a strong lamb. If for an hour or two the ewe roams away, she never makes a good mother and the lamb becomes an orphan. What happens in the human newborn when it is yanked into the air and has no mother to nuzzle it, no bare skin to cuddle against, no nipple to poke at and sleep beside until the exhaustion of birth recedes? What sort of birth is it for the mother to watch her baby being taken away? A mother can stand a lot of risks less serious than that. A lamb can stand a lot of risks less serious than this deprivation. Human mothers and babies suffer from this disowning for a long time in unvoiceable ways. No one speaks up in protest except the natural mothers of other countries and a few lucky women in our own.

The prestigious obstetrician has adopted many useful techniques. But he has made a technique out of something natural and exciting, and in many cases has degraded birth by considering it a boring but lucrative inconvenience. The successful obstetrician often lets his nurses and residents work the long hours and do the worrying. Everyone in this powerful and honored profession can call to mind just such persons and practices!

Obstetricians have a vested interest in births and pregnant women. They ought to have. Obstetrical departments of medical schools have a vested interest in them also. It takes many births to train a doctor for the unusual emergency, the surgical interference. Patient-oriented, conservative, tinkering with vital processes, moralistic, most of them are disqualified from solving or wanting to solve the population problem on a long-term basis. This has not been their task. Yet contraceptive fashions and policies are set by obstetricians for hospitals and medical societies at the county level in each state. This is truly madness in methods. Up and down America it is no wonder we have babies instead of birth control!

Out-of-wedlock pregnancy is on the rise everywhere. The role of the young male in the male subculture is often overlooked. He has been expected to seek intercourse, to boast about it among his peers, and to be callous to the emotional needs of his young partner. The condom is the only method available to the male, but it is least suited to the inexperienced. In the midst of excitement, it must be placed over the erect shaft of the penis, space must be left at the tip, and the rim of the condom must be held in place during withdrawal to prevent the sperm from spilling. Control and motivation beyond the average are required for this method to be successful. If a contraceptive vaginal foam is also used by the girl the chances of preventing pregnancy with the condom are greatly improved.

Contraceptive services exclude the unmarried minor in most communities. Few obstetricians will touch her without parental consent. This is a confusion of population goals with moral goals. Prevention of births by contraception or abortion is one type of job. Prevention of births by preventing intercourse is another type of job. The unwed minor who goes to a contraceptive clinic or dares to ask the family doctor is already a dropout from chastity. What sort of goal is served by closing the medical door in her face?

When pregnant should she be counseled to have the child? To keep it? To get married to the father? To adopt it out? Is it for some good purpose that we enforce these pregnancies? Seriously? Or are we *punishing something*, which turns out to be the child? Pregnancy and the risk of pregnancy will not just go away. But they are two different events, requiring different behavior from us.

A good salesman turns his uncollected bills over to a bill collector, and goes right on selling autos to new prospects who are likely to buy and pay for them. It is not his job to harangue the delinquent customer. His job is to go right on picking customers and selling as hard as he can. Similar hard effort should be put into sex education and family life counseling beforehand, without scolding the dropouts.

The bill collector makes a living dealing with the facts of delinquent bills. He patches up bad situations. He can sometimes keep trouble from happening again. Nobody admires his job much, but it is socially constructive. If doctors were free to deal as honestly with the dropouts from chastity, minors would benefit, and society's aims would be much better served. But about this everyone is still twice-minded! In the minds of moralistic people, enforced pregnancy is still regarded as a deterrent to "bad behavior".

The young girl brought up on "Sock-It-To-Me" buttons needs to be listened to. She may have been sexually active since the age of fourteen. Her mood is expressed in songs and happenings. Condemning a whole subculture out of hand does not reach the pregnancy problem alive in it. For one thing these ignorant youngsters are often pursuing a path that has its own sensitivity. They claim that even to think about contraception beforehand is to ruin the spontaneity of first love and to put something calculated and unpleasant into the situation. Many older men and women have felt the same thing when confronted with the facts of diaphragm and condom and the unwanted child. These methods are madness where idealism still runs high—as it does in many unspoiled parts of the world. In America, the so-called precocious young are quite direct in acknowledging their pleasure in sex, their idealism about it and their distaste for these methods. It is not their actions which are so upsetting but their openness. To stop at two, these methods are not effective enough. They are not joyful enough. The only cultures that could settle for them on a permanent basis are puritanical and hypersanitary, where pleasure and beauty are not meant to be a part of the sexual act.

Fortunately there have been two breakthroughs in technology of birth control since World War II. They came to the marketplace about the same time; they have nearly equal and very high effectiveness. Both were pioneered by obstetricians. But they have met very different fates at the hands of the medical profession and the marketplace.

The IUD or Intrauterine Device

This remarkable method of birth control has had a strange history. It may be one of the most ancient. Camel drivers in the Gobi placed smooth stones in the womb of female camels to keep them barren during long caravan journeys. Flemish midwives placed rolls of flax or linen thread in the womb right after childbirth to prevent another pregnancy. In California at the turn of this century, doctors knew about and used gold intrauterine rings for birth control. Such rings acquired a folklore value and were passed from mother to daughter. Gold pessaries and plugs for the mouth of the womb also were made about the same time with more unfortunate results. The spring arms of the pessary pressed into the tissue inside the mouth of the womb causing erosion, sometimes giving rise to infection and bleeding. The bad name deservedly given to all forms of spring or button pessaries slopped over onto the entirely different IUD and by 1935 both went out of whatever American use they had. But in other parts of the world interest in the ring and the pessary survived. In both Israel and Japan long-term studies were begun on the IUD.

It was not until 1959 that the fine work of Ishihama in Japan and Oppenheimer in Israel was scrutinized by Americans. Studies began again in this country. Meantime, plastic had come to the marketplace, especially many types of inert, flexible materials which reshaped themselves after stretching, in what was called "plastic memory". An IUD for mass use was suddenly possible.

To insert a rigid metal ring, surgical procedures had been necessary. The tight canal at the mouth of the womb had to be relaxed before a ring could be slipped in place. Dr. Lazar Margulies at Mt. Sinai Hospital in New York City and others under him experimented with the new materials. A hollow plastic straw with a plunger was finally patented and the Gynecoil, a stiff nylon spiral with a beaded tail was designed to uncoil in it. Plastic could not be boiled so cold iodine solution was used to sterilize the devices. Fed into the sterile straw with surgical gloves, the spiral unflexed into a tiny straight line. The tube and device slipped gently through the narrow cervical canal. Then the spiral was pushed out to recoil in the womb. The plunger and straw were withdrawn. Such a device could be left in place indefinitely. Any doctor could insert it in office or clinic. The first practical IUD was born. The inserter was a brilliant basic idea. The spiral device with beaded tail was not perfect. But it was successful as a method of birth control beyond expectations. It was cheap, one-shot, simple and with a high rate of preventing pregnancy. This method would have spread from doctor to doctor like a grassfire as the greatest of breakthroughs, except for one little thing—THE PILL.

The Pill

The pill was revolutionary in two ways. It really did prevent pregnancy, and in pill-taking America it could be talked about in company. Discussion of birth control came into the open in press and radio, and advertising spread from medical journals to national magazines.

From the commercial point of view, the pill had a tremendous advantage over the IUD. It had to be taken every day for twenty days each month. It was made from plant hormones in a process requiring careful and expensive controls over production. Both factors promised Syntex and the drug companies obtaining licenses a very profitable product. The woman happy on the pills is a permanent customer. She returns not only to the doctor who writes the prescriptions but to the drugstore that fills them. There is a black market in pills. There is a huge overseas demand. Finally the U.S. government itself began large-scale pill programs abroad.

A year on the pills can cost anywhere from ten to thirty dollars depending upon the women's source. This is truly an American-type product, a mere nothing in the budget of the average family, especially compared to the cost of a child. Yet it is entirely beyond reach of the world's poor.

To the user, constant cost of the pills is a major disadvantage. Repeatedly having to take them is a medical and emotional disadvantage. Long-term use of estrogen hormones is known to increase the incidence of cancer in experimental animals. Yet from the very beginning of pill research, we realized that the safety of a systemic hormone, taken regularly, in small amounts, over years, could not be tested beforehand in any reasonable way. We could only uncover the facts by permitting wide use over a long time—once the short-term risks seemed reasonable. In the same way we could not predict beforehand that we would settle and develop North America, in spite of its risks, or that the plane and the car would stay dangerous but become indispensable. Pills were adequately studied so far as research itself could provide the answer. The test would be in long-term human use. We can expect to hear from time to time reverberations such as those that percolated out of England and stirred up the American press in late 1969 and early 1970. We know the risks and the high costs of pregnancy. We are still exploring the risks and high costs of pills.

Hazards of the Pill

The pills are powerful hormones circulating through the entire body. Contraindications to use of the pill are a long list, as anyone may read in the Warnings to Physicians. Side effects felt by patients taking them are another long list.

While pill-forgetting is the biggest hazard to the user, ignorance is next. A black market exists in pills. Stealing by teenagers in America is widespread. If only a simple flyer describing the pill in street language could be stolen along with them!

What would happen to the unwed could not be worse than what is happening now. In our present system a girl cons a prescription from a married friend. She divvies it up with her friends and they return the favor until they all run out together. Pregnancy, abortion, trauma and ignorance are fostered by our officious screening of contraception from the young. Neither safety nor morals are being served. Pills might as well be purchased without prescription at the drugstore. But the instant official reaction to such glaring need is to tighten up prescriptions, and deepen the ignorance! In 1970 the enlightened state of Massachusetts imprisoned William Baird for daring to explain to unmarried college students the use of contraceptives. In the context of today this *is* absolute madness in methods.

How to Take Those Stolen Pills

Oral contraceptives should be taken at least twenty days of every month and restarted not more than seven days later. Brand switching is a cause of pregnancy in the underground, so this rule of thumb applies to most 2 mg., one-colored pills— Ortho-Novum, Norinyl, Enovid. For the young woman uncertain of her supply these compounds are similar enough to switch off, provided there is no gap in taking them. Sequentials are two-colored pills, not suitable to interchange with more common pills. They contain two different drugs designed to follow each other. Then there are other two-colored pills where only the longer series contains the preventive hormone and the short series is, in such packages, *not a dose preventing pregnancy at all*. If such pills are taken to replace Enovid or Ortho-Novum or Norinyl, they will lead to pregnancy. So beware! Read the label! Find out what you get! Ask a pharmacist or a biology teacher or a nurse or a doctor. Don't mess around with pills unless you have to, and if you have to, get them straight. One month on, one month off, because you aren't having any is a sure way to get pregnant. Get on them and stay on them or give up the whole thing and FORGET it!

What Do Pills Do?

Pills prevent a woman from producing an egg. A woman is designed to shed at least one egg every month. But during pregnancy natural body hormones prevent release of an egg. So taking a dose of the same kind of hormone all through the month prevents an egg being shed. Every month also the womb wall thickens up with tissue in case it is needed to receive a pregnancy. This womb wall would go right on thickening and then cause a dangerous breakthrough bleeding. So the pills are stopped for just long enough each month to peel down this thickening of womb tissue. Then, before an egg can get free, pills have to be started again. Every month, on time, without fail. The basic pills do one job. Stopping them and restarting them does another. Both are needed.

Doctors and nurses explain all this to women who have admission tickets to American medicine. But the men and women who need to know it most will not read this book, will not talk to anyone, and don't have those tickets. They are the ones whose funeral tab is picked up by the city, or whose children are fostered out at a public cost of $20,000 per child to age 18. Madness in methods!

But the American medical profession, Planned Parenthood and government clinics took to the pills. Hormones are fascinating to study, chemically and medically. Furthermore, not only is a prescription cheaper for the clinic than an IUD insertion, but the pills were advertised as 100% *effective if taken as directed*. Women believed this. They flocked to the method. The IUD was quickly eclipsed so that by 1968, the Health, Education and Welfare tabulation of Maternal and Infant clinics in America reported the ratio of pill patients to IUD patients as 4.3 to 1.

Why?

The doctor in clinic or practice concerns himself with the patient. Her unplanned pregnancy is his disaster. Her side effects upset him. He has been taught to worry about loss of blood. He has no public health training, nor time to collect and screen records. He may despise them. His patient is the highly excitable Mrs. Jones at the end of his telephone. No use telling *her* that she is one of the 2% of women for whom the IUD fails while still in place! Pill advertising on the other hand claims 100% effectiveness if taken as directed. So, if pregnant, she failed to take them as directed! This pregnancy was not the fault of the pill or the doctor, but of the woman. Eight million American women, their doctors and nurses have accepted this obvious distortion of the facts.

All failures of a method result in a pregnant woman. She gets just as pregnant if she forgets the pills, or if she tires of nausea and suddenly stops taking them. This is a failure of the pills for her. If the IUD falls out and she gets pregnant, it is a failure of the IUD just as much as the pregnancy with the IUD in place. The real measure of failure rate is how many woman who begin the method become pregnant by the end of the year.

When patients first start on these two methods, the rate at which the pills and the IUD fail is about the same: one to three pregnancies per 100 women on them for a year. But over time, difference shows up. Patients stay longer on the IUD. Failures with the IUD decrease steadily with months of use. At the end of five years, a group of women on the IUD will have produced measurably fewer children than a similar group started on the pills. Furthermore, the IUD seems to attract to itself the most fertile women in a population. The net births prevented is suspected to be higher by this factor.

Studies of the IUD are of exceptional quality. All of them have been done by universities and research institutions through prominent hospitals or clinics. They are of superior design and controlled follow-up. Follow-up is clinical shepherding. In a flock of sheep if one ewe is lost at lambing time you do not know her outcome; whether she died, the lamb died or both are flourishing. Yet if you are measuring pregnancies at the rate of 1 to 3 per hundred women, you cannot lose track of even one woman. Loss-to-follow-up is the greatest research expense, especially in America with our continually moving population.

This is one reason why large comparison studies of the pill with the IUD have not yet been made in this country. Studies matching pill users with IUD users in age and number of children and education are even more exacting to carry out. Only now are we beginning to receive good documentation of what has been clear since 1966. For the highly fertile woman, for the young woman just beginning her reproduction, for the poor and the ignorant, the IUD is a superior method of birth control, especially for the long pull. The IUD sits quietly in the uterus minding its own business. There are hardly any medical reasons not to try the IUD. An existing local cancer of womb or cervix, existing pregnancy or active infection are the only real contra-indications to insertion. With the IUD in place numerous common disorders of body function, diabetes, high blood pressure, other cancers, phlebitis, fluid retention, kidney disease can all be handled as usual. Yet when obstetricians get together to talk about the "management of contraception" for such patients, the IUD is rarely what they talk about!

Side effects of the IUD are bleeding and cramping. After two months in most cases, neither recur, although the monthly flow may be heavier and last longer. Women are accustomed to this type of bleeding. Cramping is also familiar. Again, the known side effects of the pill are a long, serious printed list!

"Iron-Poor Blood" and the IUD!

In India where haemoglobin levels as low as 7 grams are not rare, the bleeding caused by the IUD is very serious. Poor diet low in iron, a depleted soil, and high levels of intestinal worms and enteric diseases combine against the successful use of present IUD designs. Concentrated attack upon IUD bleeding by doctors who have pioneered and defended this method should yield prompt results. We have much more to gain and much less to spend in perfecting the IUD than in continuing to mess with estrogen hormones in implants and injections, which have all the risks, except forgetting, of the present hormone pills. IUD success could give India one of the best methods imaginable for her conditions. Early and sustained risk of pregnancy is coupled for the Indian women with low understanding of reproduction, and absolute lack of privacy or sanitation as we understand it. Condoms and diaphragms are discouraging to think of. More is known about the Indian poor than about our own poor, but similarities are suggestive. Steady motivation and an unbroken supply of pills are conditions not to be met with among the impoverished women of any country.

In India in 1969, the U.S. government had just begun an enormous pill project. It was being swept along by USAID and companies like Searle of India. But my friends among the workers in the slums and individuals in AID were sceptical. A monsoon interruption of even one cycle means a pregnancy, which makes the whole year's effort useless. In a monsoon, an in-situ IUD is better protection than a pharmacy across the river! One cannot imagine a delivery and supply system which would keep twenty million monthly cycles flowing to the villages and slums of India. But twenty million women is a low target for a nation of 600 million souls. By the end of a year, an IUD program of only two million a month would protect the same number of women indefinitely. Yet in the jungle of bureaus in New Delhi and Washington, few seem to be thinking along the lines of perfecting and "selling" a "bloodless" IUD. From Chile, however, comes refreshing new research. Adding copper to the IUD quiets the uterine tendency to cramp and lessens bleeding. Copper is a definite cell toxin also, which may reduce the few pregnancies occurring with the IUD in place.

We have everything to lose and little to gain by offering

abroad a program we have no intention of adopting at home. Until we in America cut down our population which takes 60% of the world's goods for 8% of the people, our motives will be suspect. Dr. Abraham Stone started the rhythm method in India. It was a disaster because rhythm is a disaster. We started the IUD program, which fell victim to both just and unjust criticism, equally destructive. We have backed the pills, which are rumored to increase cancer. The only homegrown program for India is vasectomy, and for this reason it may be the only success. But for demographic impact it must come before a man sires three children and in India this may be below twenty years of age!

An IUD which causes little bleeding, and an iron therapy that was cheap and quickly effective, is a combination that our research should develop for all poor women everywhere. Lowering the already low prognancy rate from insitu failure or expulsion of the present IUDs is a research project with little demographic effect. But cheap and successful control of the common experience of extra menstrual flow would have great impact on the birth rate. Menstrual bleeding means ritual exclusion from housework and child raising in many Asian countries. Other groups observe sexual abstinence during such flow. But because women are not consulted about how money shall be spent, much of the 1969 budget of $50 million from USAID went to?—pill companies! For more research into?—hormones!

The Commercial Problem

Why is it that Americans do not realize all this? Partly because the pill in America became a hundred-million-dollar business in 1968 and has been growing ever since. But partly because of the patent on the IUD inserter. The major IUD patent dates back to 1962, and was given to Dr. Lazar Margulies who devised the inserter. The hollow plastic tube with plunger is used to insert all designs of flexible IUDs. Dr. Margulies turned over the patent to Mt. Sinai Hospital where he did the work. At the urging of Dr. Alan Guttmacher, the patent was transferred (terms unknown) to the Ortho company, maker of other contraceptives and part of the huge combine of Johnson & Johnson. The excuse was that only "such a large company" could afford the costs of introducing and marketing the IUD.

In 1963, Syntex granted a pill manufacturing license to Ortho, which then marketed Ortho-Novum in 10 mg. and later 2 mg. doses. Conflict of interest was immediate. Every IUD inserted lost a much more lucrative customer for the pills. Why the Justice Department has not intervened is curious.

By 1965, due to worldwide interest of research institutes, the Lippes loop was shown to be the best available design of IUD. Many careful studies were reported by the Population Council. Dr. Lippes brought his loop to the general market using a hollow tube inserter. Deseret of Utah was enjoined from selling one like it, on suit by Ortho. Ortho then offered to buy out the Lippes loop. In the background hovered the shadow of probable infringement by Dr. Lippes of the inserter patent bought by Ortho prior to Ortho's entry into pills. Unhappily, under this threat, Dr. Lippes sold the loop to Ortho in 1965. At the time of sale, the output of loops in the local factory near Buffalo, New York employed fourteen women in the tying on of the nylon strings. In 1968, after three years of the "marketing" of Ortho, only four women were so employed.

Why Mt. Sinai sold the inserter patent outright to a huge pill company instead of licensing it contingent on sales, is a mystery. Why Ortho bought out the loop is less of a mystery. It has suppressed, not promoted the IUD. Why Dr. Lippes sold to Ortho which by that time was already hugely involved in Ortho-Novum, is the greatest mystery of all. For he was urged to fight the patent and market the loop himself, or sell to a company not involved in the oral contraceptives.

Although the IUD has been the subject of some of the best studies, it has none of the press or the public needed to make it a commercial success. If Mt. Sinai had sold the inserter patent to duPont, or a maker of surgical supplies; if Lippes had sold the loop elsewhere, IUDs might be on an entirely different footing in America. And so might contraception.

While we find a softer IUD to reduce bleeding, we should find a softer inserter, too, so that one woman can insert it simply into another. In most parts of the world, babies are born at home with another woman to help, and abortions are performed by one woman for another. Why are we so strange in what we will admit and permit? Why are we so scornful of the abilities of ordinary women to deal with these problems with a minimum of training? Given iodine solution and softer IUDs and inserters, masses of paramedical housewives could solve the population problem around the world. With less death and trauma than we have now!

For there is an ultimate madness in the IUD method also. On a worldwide basis there is no plan to get it to all the women who need it. It is not medically practical, here or abroad, with present procedures. So throughout the sixties, disaster multiplied around the world. In our own helpless cities like New York where the roaring cost of welfare, and wage demands were openly designed to break the bank and cause total insolvency, the familiar look of life merely disguised the extent of change.

Everywhere population zoomed into the new era with the old madness in methods, the one-patient orientation, the wanted-child syndrome.

Even now, the scarce doctor stands at the point of service. No method which can be mobilized on a community basis has even been seriously investigated; no program like TB X-rays or fluoridation of water supply. No cadres of non-medical people are being taught the simpler techniques of IUD insertion, abortion and vasectomy which certainly do not require twelve years of higher learning. No urgency shines from laboratory or think-tank. No massed research, no demand, no funds. Madness in method seems quite sane to the leaders from a past generation. But we will look back on this decade when there was time to do something, and money to do it with, and relative peace, and wonder what kind of madness we were suffering from, that we did not get up and demand an answer, and go discover it.

Abortion

Abortion is the commonest method of birth control in the world today. It is also a natural event which interrupts the nine months of pregnancy at any time when the foetus or the placenta connecting it to the mother fails. Far from being a tragedy, in most cases abortion is a good thing, preventing a defective embryo or faltering mother from carrying a hopeless condition to full term. It conserves energy and weeds out most of the mistakes of development. Such a device is adaptive, protecting the strength of the mother and the quality of the offspring. It is a gross misdirection of medical research to seek reduction of this natural harvest of the foetus, which for thousands of years has protected the quality of human beings.

But not all the adversities faced by mother and infant today are physical. The infant is born into a social situation also, and many risks to mother and child come from hunger, illness or hatreds of other people. The womb and its protective abortion mechanism cannot protect from these. But from early times, the human mother has done so. She is unique among females in being able to look ahead and to calculate the risks of a social situation. Self-induced abortion is an extension by the mother of the womb's spontaneous protective mechanism. Abortion was probably one of the first operations women attempted on themselves and is still the most common. All over the world it is still the most effective method of population control.

In spite of the gory stories told about self-abortion, it is natural and simple and carries reasonable risk *if* the state of the womb and its capacities are once thoroughly understood. The pregnant womb is thin and easily punctured, like a slightly thick balloon. Deep in the vaginal opening the mouth of the womb is extremely narrow surrounded by a tough ring of muscle. Into this narrow opening women have had other women insert all kinds of burning solutions and sharp instruments, with disastrous outcomes. But the embryo is a small disc of growing tissue attached to the wall of the womb. It becomes enclosed in a sac and acquires a distinct stalk by the eighth or ninth week after the first missed period. At this point, careful loosening of the membrane is quite practical. The womb expels the product and contracts to stop bleeding by the same mechanism which protects it when an embryo of this age aborts without help. Two techniques are commonly used.

Slipping a sterile finger through the dilated cervix and running it gently over the inside surface of the enlarged womb usually gets things going. This technique is sometimes used in Japan and Switzerland. Variants of finger curettage are the *sterile* insertion of *sterile,* soft rubber catheters, packs, moisture-absorbing materials, all of which cause the embryonic tissue to detach. Normal actions of the womb then take over to expel the tissue. Self-induced abortions require completely sterile technique. A sterile, flexible material is placed in the womb for twelve hours and then removed. Patience is needed until the week or ten-day process of breaking off and shedding-out is completed. Throughout this time, taking body temperature detects most infections. No hospital attention is required for abortions which make use of natural function, which maintain sterile technique, and protect the thin and delicate nature of the womb wall. For the ignorant and rough, infection and massive bleeding are serious risks. Sterilizing with dilute (orange) iodine solution and gentle use of limp materials avert these risks. When either serious bleeding or infection does occur, the nearest hospital emergency ward is obliged to give care.

These facts are smothered by the medical and legal professions who rarely permit any instruction of women in self-abortion. But women in California have been teaching self-abortion, and poor women everywhere have had nothing else.

The American medical profession has been using the steel scraper or curette, a medieval invention. Fortunately for the future, suction abortion was developed in Czechoslovakia, and is finally being used in many United States hospitals and clinics. It is an excellent technique which gently plucks off the attached tissue, without damaging the womb lining. Bleeding and risk of infection can be much reduced. This great step forward can be routinely available in the office and clinic, getting abortion not only out of the illegal back room but out of the hospital and obstetrical department. Again, many lawyers and doctors still oppose this progress.

Japan and some countries in Europe view unwanted pregnancy as a threat to the other children, the mother and the country. We in America are coming toward this, realizing ever more deeply that protecting life and its quality is more complex than we thought. Enforcing nine months of pregnancy and a lifetime of parent-child relations with all its vistas for destruction is a serious matter. Enforcing it against the will of mother and father who seek an abortion is barbaric—one of the last stands of ecclesiastic interference in other peoples' bedrooms. Slowly, surely, we will recognize the larger-than-human wisdom which designed the female womb not only to carry but also to lose a baby, and we will learn to accept it at that.

Sterilization

Sterility comes to us all sooner or later if we live long enough. It, too, is a natural event which prevents the young from having parents too old to raise them. A mother must carry the child and nourish it for nine months, and must be strong enough after birth to feed it for a year or more. If her children are to be vigorous, she ought to be a vigorous animal herself. Thus it is natural that women come to the end of childbearing and lactation long before old age.

The male, performing the stressful but brief act of mating has no further physical strain comparable to pregnancy and lactation. He remains fertile much later into life, provided he escapes serious disease.

Again, modern society by extending the length of life and by lightening the stress of pregnancy and lactation, at least for the well-to-do, has threatened ancient balances. Both men and women can become physical parents long after it is socially desirable for them to do so. At present, financial and emotional limits upon families have become severe just when biologic controls have relaxed. Thus surgical sterilization is a protective measure which can end the bearing and begetting of children as soon as these activities become socially disvalued. In the effort to redress the balance between people and resources, sterilization is the most permanent weapon we have and the least understood.

Surgical sterilization cuts the pipeline from ovary to womb, from testis to penis, so that neither egg nor sperm can make their usual journey to the site of fertilization. Surgical sterilization does not alter the rhythm of menstrual cycles nor the ripening of eggs. It does not halt the production of sperm in the testis. The basic sexual drive for both men and women is hormonal. The hormone level is not affected by this surgery. Male hormones flow from the testis into the bloodstream to the rest of the body. They are not discharged into the pipeline to the penis. Female hormones from ovary and womb also flow into the bloodstream, and never did flow appreciably into the cavity of the tubes or the womb.

Confusion and fear block wider use of sterilization and prevent happier attitudes toward it. Because sexual joy and sexual power are very important to males, vasectomy seems threatening to them when not understood. Males want to erect and ejaculate frequently, with confidence in their desirability to a woman while doing so! A sterile passionate man is free to be lover, provider and companion to a woman without enforcing pregnancy upon her. But he can create this image only if they both share a healthy attitude. Sexual effectiveness can be blocked if the man believes himself mutilated, damaged, sexually lessened or castrated. It is revealing that a sterilized woman has little of this sort of fear. Men have been sterilizing women for years. Also the woman has a monthly flow to remind her of her female hormones and ritual femininity. This is more obvious and reassuring than anything available to the male.

Furthermore, where communication is good between generations, young women may know very well that after menopause their older relatives were even more passionate and passionately desired. A tubal ligation leaving the ovaries intact is far less of a change than menopause and not usually feared by young women.

The male, too, has periodic building-up of seminal fluid and feels pressure to ejaculate but is less reassured. He often believes wrongly that the volume of ejaculate will be much less when there are no sperm in it. But the volume of packed sperm is relatively low—less than 10%—and loss of this small volume is not noticed in ejaculation. Some men even wonder if they can reach climax and ejaculate at all. Much more open discussion of such fears would change many attitudes. Young people in school are especially eager for discussion.

Today, when man or woman has had the socially desirable limit of two children, even if they are young, sterilization should be regarded as a wise and happy procedure.

But delivery of this service on a massive scale is costly at present. Delivery of it at ages young enough to affect population rates is not yet popular.

Sterilization, unlike abortion, has always been legal in most states. But the woman has only changed one set of restrictions for another. In most hospitals, tubal ligation is still under the control of a local review committee which permits few. The Joint Commission on Accreditation of Hospitals is a national body which takes great interest in the number of and grounds for sterilization. Hospitals use fear of this board as an excuse. The right to privacy, the right of a couple to decide whether they should be parents or not in this exacting society does not influence these medical custodians. There is no question here of policing medical quality or medical judgments. Such committees merely reflect the community's outdated desire for control, and permit them to interject their own natalist and puritanical moralities.

Liberal groups fighting so hard to repeal abortion laws should take a look at legal tubal ligation. Women are doomed to disappointment unless the medical review committee is challenged as a system. One or two court cases with damages will be necessary before the stubborn practice dies away. For in rural communities these are a natural stronghold of reaction. Today the best hospitals are carrying more than their share of fertility control at present. The average hospital must be quickly brought to carry its own load. Catholic hospitals even when publicly funded carry almost none. No change will happen until we realize that at present, birth control means sterilization and abortion, contraception and abstinence, on massive scales, for entire nations. And it means the difference between life and total death.

Voluntary Family Planning

16

WHY IS THE PRODUCING public making no response if we now have a population problem of such disastrous proportions? The answer is simple! Americans do not sense any disaster. They believe it may happen to other peoples, but not to them!

In 1930, the birth rate in the United States fell to 18 per thousand, long before convenient methods of contraception were available. Births fell because people in the great depression could not afford, did not *want* children. Even Americans respond to adversity. The hardship of an extra mouth to feed was real. What did those depression parents do, one wonders? Diaphragm and condom are unlikely to have produced so much demographic impact. Couples also practiced withdrawal and living apart.

For twenty-five years after World War II the American public felt no hardship. It takes effort to prevent women from having children. They are programmed to have them and they did. Throughout the fifties our birth rate hovered between twenty-two and twenty-four per thousand. Even after marketing of the IUD and the pills, wide use of these methods did not return the birth rate to eighteen per thousand until the end of the sixties. There is one striking difference between 1930 and 1969, however. There are *millions* more American women to produce eighteen babies per thousand.

Throughout the decade of the sixties, world population was considered a major crisis. But there was little response from the young American girl. Instead it was a lavish decade. Approval of birth creates an emotional glow which blocks the mother from translating the crisis of the outer world into personal fears and feelings. Competition for grandchildren is an acute illness of forty-year-old men and women in America. Against their rich encouragements, no mere discussion will be effective. The young mother must experience deep in herself the need for fewer births, and bring it down to her own behavior. She has had no feedback in America to tell her the world is crowded. She feels no threat. Girls and boys in middle-income families are still expecting to have three and four children. National and world crisis has failed to come home to them as it must, as it will.

This failure is the predictable outcome of voluntary family planning. Voluntary family planning is not a population policy nor anything like it. It is the outcome of Margaret Sanger's compromise with the Catholic Church forty years ago. At that time the infant birth-control movement had to guarantee to the church that patients would have "free choice" of methods, and their "rights" to have children would be respected.

Today this compromise is subverting our real freedom in America. It no longer bears any relation to the facts. Catholics are aware of the disasters caused by too many children and are using birth control for the same reasons as anyone else. Therefore it is high time to question what we mean by voluntary family planning and the "right" to have children. It is not a right independent of other rights, and a right to have children is not a duty to have them. A "voluntary family planning program" can be highly structured and effective like Japan's; or it can exist like the one in America with hardly any effect on population at all.

"Every child a wanted child" is still the popular slogan of Planned Parenthood. Under this banner different religions and social theories have sought common ground. The slogan endeared itself because it has a disarming sound, even to opponents of birth control. Now it has become an article of faith and figures largely in Planned Parenthood advertising. It sounds liberal and responsible and has been good for raising money.

But today it is disastrous. Because we cannot have all the children we want. Nobody can.

"Want" is a suspect word. It takes energy and responsible attitudes not to "want" children. Natural carelessness alone is enough to "want" them. Between one mother and the next, "wanting" draws no adequate distinction. Furthermore, wanting the children already born is a social imperative. Parents must pretend to love and want their children whether they do or not. It is an article of faith that Catholics want children, and Catholic children are wanted. But it is a fact that Catholics have been *taught* to want large families and are lectured into having them. Thus wanting is a treacherous measure of how many children ought to be born. What joyousness might be coming into the world if Catholics were teaching people *not* to have children!

A policy of every child a wanted child does not mention either population control or self-control. It is less a policy than an abdication of one. It accepts the mother's desire for births as absolute, disregarding her life circumstance. It ignores her limited perspective on the population problems of her country. It gives her no guidance on what to want. It offers human parents no substitute for the biological controls they have been deprived of. Worse, it disregards the increasingly frightening fact that what the mother wants or can afford will *not* be the cogent factor in the life of that child. Whether his community wants him and can afford him is the bitter question. Every child a wanted child is a natural slogan for politicians. The unwanted child has an ugly sound and is an ugly fact. Thus the nice argument runs, there should be only wanted children. To this unfinished task Planned Parenthood should set itself and its clinics. It should make every effort to prevent the unwanted.

But it does not take aim even at its own target with urgency or effectiveness. Contraception, abortion, and sterilization together can indeed prevent unwanted births. Contraception alone has *never* been able to do so.

In the past, voluntary family planning has said in effect, "Try contraception if you want to, but don't ask us for help if it fails."

This is quite literally the legal condition under which all clinics have operated.

Sterilization and abortion have not been part of Planned Parenthood service. They are not yet a part of public health. They are in most places still measures for the rich, denied to the poor. Today, Planned Parenthood could prevent unwanted births for its clinic population by providing suction abortion for all contraceptive failure. This simple remedy would accomplish what research has not been able to do—make all methods 100% effective. But even where it is legal, such a target has yet to be proposed by Planned Parenthood. The paramedical training to carry it out has not been designed by any of our fabulously costly medical schools or government health agencies.

Clinics across the nation do not hesitate to capture and lecture clinic patients from twenty to forty minutes on the merits of all the methods ever known. This protects their "freedom of choice." But it is totally dishonest in protecting them from pregnancy. Some methods are better than others and some are no longer worth using. Teaching falls apart altogether when we come to the much more critical decision, "Is this child necessary? Do you need it?"

There is no protocol for asking these questions. There are no guidelines for answering them. In the ordinary medical clinic where at present population has to be controlled, no mention of population is made. How can we say to the mother of two, "Take your iron and drink milk," and yet not say, "Have you thought of going to school or to work instead of having another child, because two is enough?"

If the issue is never raised, then the clinic certainly cannot be accused of coercion. BUT! This decision is of far greater human importance than deciding on diets and methods of contraception.

Neither will the young woman in a private office get a discussion of her role in population growth. She will be slapped on whatever method the harried doctor is using at the moment. She will be told if it fails, "But you can afford another child!"

The young woman who is poor and must visit a clinic has none the less need to understand that three and four children are a large family, that two is enough. She needs to know that, far from being criticized, she will be respected and envied for having a small family. She needs to understand why even good husbands walk off from too many children. A clinic she cannot get to, a method she cannot use, a decision she has no grasp of are all too often the lot of the poverty mother. Under the guise of freedom of choice and voluntary family planning, she is given no insight into choices at all. Our national programs will have to prevent the unwanted child and many a wanted child as well.

To permit public health departments to adopt the attitudes and errors of Planned Parenthood which have already proved so costly is absurd. It is madness in methods! Births are an epidemic and leadership to deal with epidemics ought to come from medical schools and the Public Health Service. No more voluntary families larger than two! The well-born, the smart, the rich, the educated do not need to endow the world with more than two children, because their two in the very nature of things will demand more, use up more, and pollute more than two children from the slum. These children, because their parents can afford them, are the very ones the ecosystem can least afford.

But the poor family has no need to endow the world with more than two children either. Through taxes or charity the poor child is raised as a parasite on the efforts of people not his parents. In America, for the children of the poor to flourish, there must be enough taxable couples willing to work this double load. Man is the only mammal who has worked out such a system to parasitize his own kind, but throughout nature parasitic success imposes limits of its own.

Voluntary family planning groups have a natural history. They begin small, with no funds, a vital idea and a few dedicated persons. With increasing money and success, they age. Next, larger memberships encourage delegation of projects to a nucleus group, who may retain some of the founding fire, but who also begin to include a new kind of person, oriented to acquiring personal importance. The in-group now delegates the paper work and administrative detail to paid staff. Gradually, direction and decision making are also transferred to paid staff. No matter how highly recommended paid officers may be, there is a dilution of the original intent. There are now salaries to be earned, territories to be enlarged, power to be usurped within the organization, as well as formal public purposes to be carried out. Personal importance and personal publicity overshadow decision making. The initial goal moves far down the list in daily urgency. Egotists are attracted.

In the final stages of such an organization, paid executives write all the letters, pay all the bills, arrange all the conferences and invite all the speakers. They write the publicity and suppress opposition both within the ranks and from outside. They raise their own salaries and aggrandize their own duties. In its death throes such an organization has a long list of members who know little about it; its coffers are easily filled and casually emptied. In order not to risk loss of donations, it now muffles free opinion, dodges discussion and narrows its function to a strict party line approved from above. Respectability becomes palpable, and to the activists, a little sickening.

Larger, more expensive and more formal annual dinners mark the trend. The most dedicated of the Board and the rank and file from the local chapters can do little to alter policy, to energize action. By structure and design they are cut off from information, and from each other. Their membership only lends credence to the facade masking decay. Either the dying organization endures a convulsion from within, an all-out open battle for control and redirection—or it divides. The new pioneers head off more energetically in their own directions. Today in America Planned Parenthood-World Population is undergoing both events.

Planned Parenthood has suffered from a tacit conspiracy not to rock the boat, to keep funds flowing from private donors, industrial companies and the federal government. New projects, expensive quarters, salaries, and pensions burgeon. Yes, pensions! Now the fifth biggest volunteer health organization in the country, it is empire-building, pension-planning, developing a corporate immortality to rival any on Wall Street. Planned Parenthood has a national paid staff, getting $60,000 salaries. It has regional paid centers and paid executives earning $12,000 in many locals. Every budget has spiraled upward. Population in the news has added to funds because of the prevalent myth that voluntary family planning is population control.

Planned Parenthood is not doing a thing about population control—it never has!

No one knows this better than the doctors, public health officials and Planned Parenthood staffs who are both agents and victims of the myth. But change will not come from them. They are too comfortable. It must come from outside pressure, from an informed public sticking its nose in where it is not wanted. The job is being stretched indefinitely. Coffers are bulging. Life has never looked so good for the organization or so bad for real birth control. Voluntary family planning is relaxed family planning, well heeled, without emergency. Planned Parenthood has had no fear of failure, no genuine respect for its critics, no notion that they may be right.

This is the more exasperating, because it means that voluntary population control has never been tried in America. Although the public might rise to an emergency, it has not been roused. The public can respond to facts, but it has not had them. The lack of clear targets, of hard thinking, of tough minds has prevented Americans from trying a truly voluntary program until it may be too late. Long ago we should have had a well-mobilized effort like the polio campaign, designed to reach everyone. American parents were deeply afraid of polio, but information and leadership made them more so. Americans should be just as fearful of the unchecked growth of population in their own town, in their own county, in their own state. But information to make them so has not been forthcoming. Why? In this great free, secular country, is the forty-year-old compromise with the Catholic church still keeping us from meeting this emergency? No government supported programs aim openly at halting growth in the Catholic countries of the world. Nor in America. No such effort has been made.

Why not? Because Planned Parenthood is a monopoly and a very aggressive one. Few other organizations challenge its philosophy or its practices, although individual scholars have been outspoken. Few voices were raised in protest across the country against the narrow target of five million poor women, except the voices of demographers and militant blacks. Doctors fell for it. Racists fell for it. Upper-class leaders fell for it. Focusing on the five million women has set rich against poor, black against white, in a totally unnecessary division. For there were fifty million reproductive women in America, not five million, during the decade, 1960-70. The rich would have small families if they were not under the impression that they are paying taxes in order for the poor to have large ones. The poor would have small families if they did not think the rich were having large ones because they can afford them. Everyone could and would have small families if the urgency were made clear.

The ineffectiveness of national Planned Parenthood during the sixties is bitter, and cannot be forgiven. It has been a monopoly in restraint of trade. It has stood squarely in the way of a population policy for its own clinics, and its own clinics have blocked the development of other services. The general membership, by prolonging and condoning, has set back the clock, when every second three children are being born.

Right now the voluntary ideal is going down the drain for want of this multiple effort, this real test. Demographers and ecologists who are most alarmed about population cannot do the job because the methods used in birth control are still tied to medicine. Medicine cannot do the job because it is still bemused by voluntary family planning. The public cannot do the job because it thinks Planned Parenthood is already doing it. And Planned Parenthood is happy to let them think so.

Public officials go no further than they are forced to go, than they are directed to, so it is not any kind of solution to turn this program over to government, not at least until wide public demand exists.

Fortunately other groups are emerging on the population scene. The National Association for Repeal of Abortion Laws and the Abortion Reform Association are attacking that issue. The only difference between them is the most practicable kind of legislation. The more radical-sounding repeal law is in fact the most practical and the most conservative. Repeal removes the question of abortion from the courts and leaves it to the woman and a recognized physician, and the medical practice code, just where the law leaves all other medical considerations of life and death.

Reform laws have clogged the courts in the few states where they have passed and these states are now going for repeal. The fact that there is one abortion for every four births in America is fairly well accepted by the Association for the Study of Abortion. It is only a matter of time until early abortion is the standard outcome of contraceptive failure.

In 1968 Population Dynamics produced the break-through film, "Beyond Conception." In 1969, Zero Population Growth was started in Connecticut by a young lawyer named Richard Bowers. Paul Ehrlich, author of the *Population Bomb* helped to encourage and expand it across the country. This non-medical group is action oriented toward all projects and legislation affecting the national birth rate.

The Association for Voluntary Sterilization, or AVS, has encouraged and helped finance vasectomy and tubal ligation for many years. Their recent efforts are forcing recognition that sterilization is a valid method of birth control. For outstanding accuracy in reporting and steady influence on legislators, the Population Reference Bureau has been important over a long period. This bureau will no doubt continue to be influential in the dismantling of incentives to birth embedded in various parts of our tax and legal structure.

A large amount of foundation money has recently been shifted to the population field by the Ford Foundation and the Rockefeller Foundation's Population Council. Careful medical and demographic studies are funded and published. As a result of many influences and a growing grasp of the facts, the U.S. Congress has authorized HEW and USAID to spend some money in the field of birth control, providing for education as well as clinic service.

The Population Crisis Committee adds an urgent voice. Thus the time is right and the avenues and structures exist for an entirely new approach to the problem of stopping national growth. In the seventies there is some hope that a new approach will be made, and new voices listened to. To drop our population fast enough and far enough, American women need to get contraception, sterilization and abortion as directly as they buy food in the supermarket. But voluntary family planning, with its syndrome of case history, clinic follow-up and counseling *ad nauseam* will never do it. For the public to permit large federal programs to follow up that same alley is not absurd—it is suicide.

Lifeboat Behavior

17

VOLUNTARY POPULATION CONTROL is a very different task from voluntary family planning. To reduce population we must reach beyond the individual family and reverse the social forces which encourage having children. Many serious Americans doubt that this can be done in any voluntary way. It is certainly clear from study of animals that our population problem is complex. Instinctive reactions to density, and ecological harvesting are both trustworthy controls humans have been deprived of. Instead, we must react to a danger grasped only by the intellect, and only by handfuls of people. Our problem is further complicated because of our sexual pattern. For us, love and reproduction are never out of season. There is no natural infertile period which means contraception must be practiced around the year and around the clock. This has practical consequences in the design and use of contraceptives, and even more critical consequences when we contemplate preventing conception for twenty years or for an unwilling person. As if these physical difficulties were not enough, human beings raise religious and ethical objections which also have to be met.

No epidemic can be controlled by human measures without an energetic and perspicuous design. We can do the wrong things; we can do the right things too slowly; and in either case, the epidemic of humans will run its course, burning out in one or another of the dooms predicted for it. Nevertheless, while some despair, others are bound to try preventive measures and to pursue them.

Humane population reduction requires several steps. Accepting a limit of two children per couple is the first one, and resolving to make maximum use of our best methods of birth control is the second. Closely related to this second step is an urgent need to develop much better methods. A straightforward effort to achieve even this much would be quite effective.

Unfortunately, even perfect methods of control will not prevent births we do not in fact want to prevent. We must realize all the while that the will to solve the problem is the determining factor, and communicating this to masses of uninformed people is a major task. Even a general resolve to reduce births will not be uniform. It can come in all degrees, from lip service to complete dedication. Each one of us, seriously considering population, is being pressed to move a little farther than is comfortable, a little farther than last year. Even so, many people who admit the need, and accept the methods, find it distasteful or presumptuous to influence the behavior of others. Yet this is the third step, transforming our dubious commitment into decisive action.

Each one of us has a part to play: the druggist who determines to display contraceptives; the insurance executive who determines to cover costs of abortion; the housewife who decides against another child; the young girl who goes to job-training instead of marriage; the doctor who changes lifelong habits and takes up his share of birth prevention. Important also is the politician who listens to advocates of population and ecology control, and understands the consequences of ignoring them—all these and countless other sorts of practical people take part in producing change. Organizations can be influential also. Banks will fund new patterns of community living and industry will redesign itself to profit from lowered population and conserved resources. Churches, by placing a higher value on the quality of life and the appreciation of children can counteract the natalist forces within their structure. If populations are to be reduced by humane means, selected by ourselves, and not by war, famine and disease, then everyone will have to take part. That is the condition of success.

Once we have enlisted the public, then specific issues become important. Some will work for abortion. Some will not. Some are voluntary family planners. Others are ready to set limits and urge legislation. The difficulties which arise here never bothered animal populations! But words, their use, misuse and abuse are severe obstacles to effective human action. Just because such verbal confusion is a peculiarly civilized illness does not mean that populations cannot die of it!

Errors in our use of language are matched by serious distortions built into language itself. In English, adjectives come in contrasting pairs which tempt us to think them more separate than they are: good and evil; natural and unnatural; voluntary and involuntary. The true-false logic into which these adjectives fit is a powerful tool in mathematics, and the basis of scientific classification. We are perfectly familiar with it in many forms. As children we play the guessing game, animal, vegetable, mineral. We answer true-false questionnaires in school and in employment forms. We are aware that some of our most complex thinking is produced in the yes-no dichotomy of computer languages. Thus from an early age, powerful forces encourage us to exaggerate difference and seize upon extremes.

But we ought to be cautious. Computer programming commands some of the highest wages in industry and research, for very good reasons. The two-valued system does violence to the mixed and shifting experience of being alive. It takes great skill to translate experience from common English into accurate binary bits which can be read by electric circuits. It takes just as much skill to use the sensitive English language correctly, to reflect truthfully the many shades of living experience. Forcing us into an either-or schema in debate invokes the very distortions we need to avoid. Modern linguistics recognizes this, and gives the speaker of common language a new stature as the arbiter of what words are doing.

Once the English-speaking person has learned to use such words as right and wrong, natural and unnatural, it would be difficult to upset his usage. We expect him to learn a word, to say how he is going to use it and to use it consistently that way. The only thing we can do with his definition is to contrast it with our own, to discuss the adequacy of the criteria he used, and to make him uneasy about them. If he is using a word in a more special or more restricted way, or in a way which differs from common understanding, then modern language study shows how to document this by investigating common usage. Many a population argument could stand such an investigation!

Campaigns to change abortion laws are a good example. They run into the sentence *abortion is murder*. Investigating, we find general agreement that murder applies to the death by violence of a human being. Offspring are conceived and born. When do they become human beings? At conception? When they first kick? At birth? After surviving for a year? We find different groups upholding each of these definitions. In 1970 the California Supreme Court held that an embryo is not a human being. For abortions in the early months, we find none of the usual ceremonies of human death, no public mourning, no burial service, no masses for the dead. We do not find many indictments for abortion as murder; we find few convictions. Looking further, the penalties actually imposed for performing an early abortion are not the penalties imposed on murderers.

Linguistic analysis might look next for words like *child* or *baby* which designate a human being. In the early months we say she had a "miss" or she was pregnant and she lost *it*. We say the *baby* kicks. The Bible says great with *child*. By the time anyone is great these days, we say she is carrying a *baby*. The common language does make a clear distinction between early and late pregnancy. Just as the absence of funeral ceremonies distinguishes between abortion and ordinary death. Therefore the sentence *abortion is murder* is not a statement of fact, but an emotional claim. We waste a great deal of time in treating it like a factual statement. Reduced from a statement to a claim, it becomes like any other claim; the burden of demonstrating it falls on its supporters.

If we are going to reduce population quickly enough, we cannot afford such intractable arguments. We should recognize them as an illness and apply a remedy. The most conservative groups in America today have less than a high-school education, are over forty and are women. They are particularly vulnerable to misleading slogans. It is always useful to show these limited but sensible people how a statement of fact differs from a claim and to defuse for them the rhetoric by which they are especially influenced. Angry debate can be shifted into practical analysis of human behavior, and to the common misuse of troublesome words. Such education is a very tedious road which even educators think we have no time for. Looking at the political scene in population, it seems we have no time for anything else! Without it we will not get the solid political backing necessary to carry out projects even if we get the votes to vote them in. Many more people will take part in reducing population if we respect them enough to handle population arguments in this manner.

This is especially true of coercion. It is misleading to attempt to draw a sharp line between what is voluntary and what is non-voluntary. Every day we take part in a number of actions which fall somewhere between voluntary and compulsory. We drive on the right. We stop at red lights. Most of us pay taxes with at least enough willingness to forestall the Internal Revenue Service. Any one of us could refuse to pay taxes, could run red lights, and risk the censure, the legal sanction, or the smashup. The public at large could not be forced into any of these actions by any power but its own. We surrender some "freedoms" to do as we please in order to obtain more important ones—to drive with reasonable safety and to live in a solvent community offering facilities we could not provide for ourselves. Not so very long ago one had the "freedom" to choose whether or not to be vaccinated for smallpox. A great deal of heavy selling was required to persuade the public to support the legislation that now makes vaccination mandatory. Today far from feeling that their freedom is impaired, people accept vaccination thankfully as one of their greatest protections. This is a hopeful model for population control. Smallpox has come full circle. There has not been a case of smallpox originating in the U.S. for twenty years. The new question is how soon and how safely can we return to a voluntary program.

In their pure forms it is not difficult to distinguish between what is voluntary and what is coercive, but when these terms are applied to matters of wide public interest, they at once begin to partake of each other. Are we being coerced when we are forbidden by law to go through red lights in order that we may survive to go safely through green ones? Certainly, yes, if we define freedom as that particular kind of anarchy. Are we being coerced when all the tricks of the media are used to urge us to buy orange juice, vitamins and milk? Or are we being coerced only when the media are selling cigarettes? An honest answer has to be that the pressures are indistinguishable. Nevertheless we seem to be in general agreement that liquor and now cigarettes should not be promoted by such powerful means. Public consensus occurs prior to legislation on most issues, and such a consensus in favor of the small family could be extremely effective.

We know perfectly well that public behavior is manipulated by advertising and by prestige suggestion. The planned obsolescence of American consumer goods in the last four decades has depended upon our willingness to follow fashion. Since American family size has already dropped from eight children to three without any deliberate effort, family size is not an inherent value nor a fixed pattern. Indeed if Margaret Mead is correct, family size responds to peer pressure and is sensitive to fashion. Even if superficial and short-lived, a fad for the one-child family could be very helpful at this point while we are turning our populations around! Advertising for small families is already beginning. This is a normal use of social pressure to accomplish a desired end. Only those groups can object who do not wish small families to become the norm. Advertising attempts to obtain by fashion and consensus what fewer people are ready to obtain by law. If American advertising were to try an all-out campaign it might be very effective.

Population control is usually talked about in abstract terms, as though there really were such a technical possibility. For the time being at least, there is no promise at all of any mass method, so there can be no population control without individual birth control and individual compliance. Too often this goes unsaid. Even the most sincere demographers, urging us to stop at two fall silent when asked, How?

On the other hand, personal birth control can become effective population control only when it extends across society in an organized way. It is not enough for idealistic young couples to stop at one or two, or have none themselves. Theirs may be an important example; it directly reduces births. They feel perhaps too keenly that if the worst happens, if the ills of unchecked population swamp them and their children, they will have fewer to agonize with, fewer to suffer. For the long run, such private sacrifice merely favors breeders over non-breeders and fails to accomplish its aim. To be effective, personal population control must expand quickly into public policies.

Experts in birth-control methods have been just as blind, refusing to discuss population control while working hard to improve techniques in contraception, sterilization and abortion. The west is still caught in the absurd rationalization of voluntary family planning and "every child a wanted child".

Meanwhile the general public evades the issue of controls or becomes vituperative. On the religious front we are treated to the spectacle of celibate priesthoods busily enforcing pregnancy and childbirth on overburdened families around the world. This Freudian paradox is too peculiar to dwell on, but it does suggest a consoling thought. If it is good to have many children, it is sacred not to have any!

Face to face with uneven breeding behavior, with existing deselection and thousands of irresponsible births, we must exchange notions of voluntary family planning for population control. Enormous sums are spent by federal and state governments to encourage use of good parental stock in animal husbandry, to reduce herds and conserve the range. Yet the nastiest words in the language are hurled at anyone who tries to discuss limits or to discourage unsuitable parents from breeding. Even informed and dedicated people have failed to grapple with this issue because they have missed the role which coercion plays in everyday life.

In conditions of scarcity the civil right to have unlimited births simply does not exist. Such a claim is attention-getting and suspect. It is a favorite argument of minorities in support of their own overproduction of births. The right to have children fits into the network of other rights and duties we share and must dovetail with the rights of others. When all of us must curtail our production of children none of us has an overriding civil right of this kind. The closer we live together and the more of us there are, the fewer civil rights we can exercise before they infringe upon those of another. This adverse relation between dense population and personal freedom is easily documented around the world. It is time for people sincerely interested in civil rights to expose such special pleading, and to intervene when it is leveled against local or national programs.

Population control has yet to mobilize "nice" American women. Yet if American wives united behind a pattern of later marriage, small family size and new occupations for women, we could reduce births with unexpected speed. A new spirit is needed. Instead of indulging in superiority and dissension, women need to support and understand each other, and to energize their untapped capacities. Margaret Sanger is gone. Margaret Mead was born before 1900. Mary Calderone is a grandmother. Where are the leaders in their thirties and forties? The time is ripe for them to appear.

In America, demand for more of everything has brought more food, more housing, cars, boats, TVs, fashionable clothes, within range of poorer and poorer people. To bring a better life within the range of everyone is on the national agenda. In our industrial history technical solutions have flowed from serious demands. Demand for the small family will produce the new methods and forms of service, will produce the climate of opinion and the community effort needed. Our greatest efforts as a nation have been made when we glimpsed a new future, happier possibilities. This is what is bound to happen when we finally grasp the meaning of our present population growth. Incentives and sanctions will hustle advertising, education and research. This is not a one-shot epidemic, a one-shot cure, but a total change of human patterns for all foreseeable generations. If birth control is to remain voluntary in any sense of the word, we and the world must rapidly *demand* a pattern of small families and zero growth.

"More is better" is one of the central economic issues we are attacking. Biologically, ecologically, more humans are not better but worse, for themselves and for every aspect of the ecosystem that supports them. The economic natalist proceeds from the hard position "more humans are always better." Once that may have been true, but no longer. To convince industry, and the average working family is the heart of this conflict and the ground upon which it must be fought out reasonably among us.

If people really believe that "more is better," or that they have a civil right to produce all the children they want, what then? How are we to convince them, or to coerce them if they cannot be convinced?

There seems to be unreasonable gloom over this issue. The instinct for survival is strong in us. Truth tends to become accepted. These two forces together will move us to do something about too many people in a surprising hurry—once the breeding population feels the personal pinch. It is our rights, our space, our water and air that is being wrecked and intruded upon.

Around the world and in America we are moving from abundance to scarcity. This is an old story to human populations. It has happened before and the patterns to deal with it are well understood. Plenty of living people remember bundling paper, squashing cans, lining up for gasoline and meat. We already know what the ethics and politics must become.

This is the moment of lemmings, crowding to the edge of the sea. We are crowding our children into the lifeboat earth with hardly more perception than lemmings that this is what we are doing. Each of us wants to hand over a child, wants a place in the lifeboat for our own. Each one, having one, each couple having no more than two, expects to share in the gene pool of the next generation. Already the lifeboat is full. With more children it will be unseaworthy endangering all the rest. But along come some couples with five or six children saying, "We had a right to them. Put them aboard."

What then are the ethics of parents handing over only one or two children to the future, trusting them to the lifeboat planet which so far as we know is all there is of life in the interstellar spaces? The cruelty of the dilemma is caused by those who create more than their share in the first place. Somehow or other, the ration and the rule of the lifeboat will be enforced. We will not permit the crowding of lemmings. For the sake of all children, no one can be allowed to have more than his share. This is lifeboat behavior. Pure water, pure air, enough oxygen and a stable climate are essentials none of us know how to produce but which our mere existence in too-great numbers is enough to destroy. Once we admit this we can face up to our lifeboat situation.

The astronauts, struggling with systems failure in their spacecraft shared the tension and extra work, but also the final oxygen supply. The horrified nation, listening to their ordeal in space, did not ask aloud the final question, and no one has given the answer. If the supply was too small to get all three of them back, what was the military decision? Unequivocal orders to one of them to bring the ship back? And to others to turn off their oxygen supply? Or permission to share to the end; permission for none of them to make it. . . .

Once we recognize an emergency, we can bring to bear the ethics of scarcity and sharing. We have techniques for dealing with disaster. We can develop an orderly flow of births into— and deaths out of—the world. Resources can be in balance with the people who use them. We can recover a margin of safety in all our life systems. But we cannot have this order, this sharing, or this margin of safety until we admit we have been almost crushed in the crisis. We have no hope of systematizing a rescue until we know that we need to be rescued.

Thus we are in the midst of two very critical jobs at the same time. We have to make a luxurious nation believe it is on the brink of irreversible scarcity and damage. We have to police and self-police the country in the world which prides itself most on its personal liberty, its constitutional rights, and its love of children. We have to turn our values around one hundred and eighty degrees.

Coercion

18

In our present population dilemma, there is no perfect solution. We shall have to deal as usual with a choice of evils, and we shall be forced to accept some of them. Yet large groups still oppose this realistic approach to population control. They are behaving as though they do not have to play in this game. If they cannot play with the ground rules of completely voluntary targets and the right to have all the children they want, they will not play at all. They even take pride in this position and expect others to admire them for their principles. They are sure theirs is the American, the liberal, the democratic position. But this is not the case.

Stopping at Two ourselves does not unload the responsibility for seeing that others stop at two also. If large families are a danger to us all, we cannot permit someone else to endanger us. We are almost as much to blame for the third child we let others have, as for the third child we might have ourselves. If there is a consequent disaster, we will have been accomplices in it just the same.

Most advocates of immediate halt to population growth are sincere. They are prepared to be single or childless, to have one or stop at two themselves. Yet many of them claim to be unwilling to impose their position on others. Possibly what they fear is having such rules imposed on them. They may expect a backlash against all birth-control programs, or worse, dread some kind of federal replay of the Nazi record. These fears are respectable, but moral pretenses which hide them are not. These pretenses misread the American character and the nature of our democracy. It is not typical of Americans to accept targets for themselves that they will not impose on others. When crisis erupts, we are far more likely to rush out and help regulate others than we are to close the door and regulate ourselves.

While an ethics of scarcity exists, while births endanger all of us, we have a duty to reduce our own production of children and a right to require it of others. This duty must fall on me, not because I have conscience enough or sense enough to see it, but because the public danger allots it to me, and if to me, then to you, and everyone! If black, white, rich, poor are part of the body politic in the United States, then being black, white, rich or poor are not grounds for special exceptions. If legislation is what we require to insure that everyone will stop at two, then legislation is the prospect.

So this means we can't have a voluntary solution? NONSENSE. We *can* stop having children voluntarily all over America, all of us. Everywhere. That will do it. We can drop population quickly right away. Much the best! Just as we can stop smoking or running red lights. But we don't.

The difference between smoking which we do not yet penalize and running the red light which we do penalize, is the difference between causing private and causing public risk. When birth was a private risk to the private family, we did not need legislation. Now that birth is a public risk to all families, legislation is an option we need to face.

American political life is such that people will attack population problems, seriously implement projects, and spend money only if a legislative issue is raised. They will not otherwise take it seriously. They could—but they don't. The voluntary movement to stop at two is important; it ought to be able to attract everyone on its merits of fairness and sense. But if it doesn't?

If it isn't going to? Then, as one of my neighbors on a county road board used to say, we need reg'lation with teeth.

One by one, as individuals come to accept Stop at Two for themselves, the need to persuade and coerce others will also develop. Legislation in America is of just this nature; enough people come to agreement and enforce that agreement upon everyone. The hitch in population control and most measures proposed to deal with it, is the lack of a selfish component. For most people it simply isn't true that they value the future of their children above their own immediate pleasures or economic needs. The selfish component is missing. We stop at red lights; we accept vaccination and taxation because there is a strong selfish motive to do so; and we pass legislation to make sure everyone else complies also. Prohibition passed two-thirds of the states as a Constitutional amendment. Yet enforcement failed because for those who really liked their liquor, it offered no selfish component!

It is the sad fact that intelligent fear, informed opinion and scientific evidence are not enough to motivate us. There must also be an appeal to avarice or to personal selfishness. So far most population proposals have been too idealistic. They have not uncovered the sensitive nerve of selfishness. But there are such nerves. Obviously, we don't want to be the ones to limit our population when others aren't going to. The primitive response of both sides was to breed. The new population response is to stop others from breeding as well as to stop ourselves. Self-interest begins to operate here.

Another area of self-interest is in stable government. Those who have jobs or homes to lose in general uproar have a selfish interest in orderly change. Hungry, unruly mobs, unemployable people are the plague of crowded countries. We have every reason to reduce the cause and avoid the impasse of anarchy. It is humane selfishness to improve the quality and decrease the quantity of human life. When the story is all told, our ideals will be strongly reinforced by appeals of personal advantage.

Strategy is important. Is discussion of legislation going to spur on voluntary measures to success—or is it going to foster a heels-dug-in, damned-if-I-do approach? The life of absolutely every grandchild of people alive today is at stake. It is to be hoped that even the most refractory militant, even the most rigid natalist will cooperate in that survival program, once they understand it. The demand for social change first is an error because the logical flow of remedy is not two-way. Solution of other problems, poverty, drugs, violence, race, power-shortage and pollution will be hastened by an easing of population pressures. Population control will not be hastened by any improvement in these other problems. It must be attacked in itself, by applying a broad spectrum of correctives. We need to take out an insurance policy on the future, OUR future, by considering and discussing the three stages of mutual legislative coercion. Already some first steps have been proposed for demolishing incentives to breed.

In a natalist society like our own, the tentacles of natalist incentives and legislation are buried deep into the political flesh. To isolate and pry them loose one by one at top speed is a critical job that the press and the legal profession can accomplish. If everybody were to get a $700 tax deduction for running red lights, the rule of stopping at a red light would certainly be broken. If everybody continues to get a $700 tax deduction for third and fourth children, the norm of two will certainly be broken. So we must remove this kind of incentive if we wish the two-child norm to be obeyed as the red light is obeyed.

It is not easy to recognize natalist encouragements. We are having second thoughts about adoption homes which isolate the unwed mother and which foster out her baby sight unseen. Unless she counts this child as one of her two, the system appoints her to contribute more than her share of genes to the next generation. Merely on grounds of age and maturity, these are not the mothers a reasonable society would select to produce more than their share of births.

Although contraception should prevent these pregnancies, blocks exist and repeaters have been common. If an unwed mother cannot raise her child effectively, she should have an early abortion and defer a first birth until she can enjoy the child. Adoptive parents, aware of population, should look for orphans and deserted children and not subsidize the taking-away of first borns from young American girls.

The second level of effort seeks to replace incentives to breed with incentives and rewards for having a small family. This will sit better with the uneasy when they realize that in many ways our society has already paid and bribed people to *have* children. It is morally no worse to pay or bribe them not to, when the general good requires it.

The third level of effort sets out to penalize deliberate violations of the small-family norm, and to set up controls which prevent such violations.

First of all we demolish subsidies for the large family. The loudest objection to such a proposal is the moral-sounding sentiment, "But we must not punish the child". On the contrary, we must not punish all other children by trying to protect some. If a couple cannot meet the cost of rearing children, why should they be allowed more than two at public expense? Every child they have after two is a threat to all other children including their own. Most children in America are neither from the very poor nor from the very rich family. If a couple can afford the cost of raising children, why should we give them any tax deduction at all? Getting these natalist deductions out of the law is a two-pronged program. We need to dismantle the tax deduction which subsidizes the child of middle- to upper-income families. We need to demolish a welfare system which subsidizes more than two for the indigent. Unless both programs are placed together on the same agenda, and related to the same objective of the two-child family limit; unless both are passed with the same diligence, their impact on the welfare of all children will be lost in an uproar of special protest.

Instead of supporting all poor children with equal payments per child, we could cut the payment for each existing child and for each parent by a stated percentage at the birth of the third. If each payment were cut by 20% when the third child was born, the loss of subsidy would be in step with the loss to the national ecosystem of having to support five instead of four people. In every family not on welfare, penalty in life does fall on the older siblings when the new young are born. It does fall in fact upon the parents. So it is not unjust for loss of subsidy to reflect stepwise the facts of loss to our national well-being which is caused by that extra birth.

The middle and upper classes receive tax deductions for each additional child through college years. This is highly discriminatory. Before it can be a benefit, the income level has to be sufficiently high for college to be a prospect. So it is not an advantage to the lowest income family. It is significant, but not overriding, to the middle-income family. It is given just the same to families who would not notice $7,000 let alone $700. So let us not defend the equality and American wisdom of the present income tax deduction for children! It would be just as fair to do away with it across the board.

The bias toward births can be perceived if we contrast our present system with a base exemption of $1,200 for each individual over eighteen. At present almost 40% of our population is under eighteen. So we could almost double the current adult exemption if we dropped the exemption for children. The single, the childless would no longer be penalized for their state. Yet a couple with two children would have two of these higher adult exemptions, $2,400 between them—almost as much as the two-child family now receives. There could be nothing very objectionable in that. The disparity between these systems would continue to widen above two children, as it should when we become serious about the small-family norm.

We cannot sympathize with the eloquent sob that this penalizes the child, because today the influx of children penalizes every child.

The most obvious subsidy we give large families is unlimited free schooling. The original objective was to obtain an educated electorate. But nothing in this objective prevents us from restricting the subsidy to two children. The full per-capita cost of schooling should be borne by the family producing the third or higher child, when we analyze it carefully. The school tax does not fall on parents according to number of children, but falls on the property owner who may be single, sterile, or post-reproductive. There is no civil right to this tax base for school children. It has grown like Topsy. The poor home owner subsidizes education for the prolific rich as well as for the prolific poor. In a nation which advocates home-owning, this is strange justice indeed. It could only be justified, *it could only have happened, in a natalist society*.

If American parents paid a base sum per child for education it would not destroy democracy nor education. Far from it. It would reverse some of the natalist inequities of our present system. The financial burden would be shifted to the consuming family, where it falls in most other forms of taxation. We would still subsidize education from the general funds, possibly "matching" the parental contribution for each child. We would still be picking up the tab for the children deemed "poor". But public education would have a direct financial interest in the parent. The consuming family would not pay if they sent their child to a private school instead. Thus the school system would have direct competitors. Insensitivity to the needs and wants of the community has been the common accusation flung at schools and college administrations. If parents had something to pay, and schools had something to lose, both parents and schools would give closer attention to what they were mutually doing and expecting.

Strong emotional reaction to these proposals is probably a

good measure of the emotional investment in natalist systems, and not a measure of concern for education! Rearranging the educational burden from a bonus to a pay-for-use system is a reasonable proposal which would end major subsidy to the middle-class baby producers.

Once we remove breeding incentives from the educational system, we can devise educational rewards for the small family. One legislative proposal offers twelve quarters of state college tuition to the *only* child, or to the *second* child if it is the *last* child, of each parent. A certain number of years of state residence may be required. This type of legislation takes a relatively light bite at the problem; it does not involve large initial outlay of funds. But it would attract wide attention by its explicit purpose, and because education is dear to the American dream, it would stand a fair chance of passing into law.

The happiness of a two-child norm is not to be forgotten. It permits many people to stay single. It permits many couples to have none, who today feel forced to have a family. It encourages the only child. Parents of the only child can quickly borrow half a dozen more. After a weekend with eight, it would be great to return seven of them home again. This kind of happy plural parentage benefits both child and adult. There is greater freedom for men and women to be themselves, and for children to enjoy other adults in this newer type of society. Compared to the atomic isolation of the American family, its dog-in-the-manger attitude toward raising its children, and the cruel age-grading which is fostered by graded schools, it is greatly to be hoped for!

We have to have celebrations. If we cannot have births to celebrate, we have to find a way to celebrate non-births. Instead of lauding the Maytag twelve-child family, young clubs can recognize the longest record without a pregnancy, older ones the longest record of no more than four grandchildren. On every hand we can encourage women to develop new activities for women outside the home.

But the harsh problem begins in the third stage, when we must punish offenders, and deter them from offending. To value the freely adopted pattern of population control, we need to examine what sorts of legal coercion can be effective. Obviously we can fine and imprison offenders against the law. But that will not prevent them from having more than two children. Fines and imprisonment are not ways of enriching the social relations among us. When we have to resort to them, something has already gone wrong with our system of deterrence. None of this sort of legal compulsion seems promising for population control.

We need to press the inquiry forward with patience and regard for truth, no matter how upsetting it may be to some of the public. Overpopulation is a nasty illness, and some of the cure is bound to seem unpleasant.

We already register births. We have to have a birth certificate to belong to America. So there is half the battle of coercion. We know who has had children, and how many. When a couple want a birth certificate for a second child, they can be issued a certificate pending sterilization, or agreement to abort any subsequent pregnancy. On a wide scale, couples are resorting both to abortion and sterilization already. This is hardly a repressive law when it codifies and equalizes an existing practice.

Penalty for having a third child comes harder. We can visualize many disturbing solutions, and justifiably fear all of them. Russian truth serum, Nazi gas chambers have made us distrust the ability of governments to control their use of naked power. There is genuine abhorrence of artificial insemination, of crèche-raised children and the end of family life. But the grim pictures we can conjure up need not come true in the daytime world. Nor is the grisly experience of Russia, China or Nazi Germany reason to prohibit population control. That nightmare need not be repeated in the public decisions of democratic nations. However, one guaranteed road to failure of democratic process is the road to population explosion. To avoid that certain calamity, we may have to accept some risks in coercive legislation. What sort of punishment can we devise to fit the crime our natalist flesh tends to approve of?

Again, after the third child is born, both mother and father will have to present themselves at the hospital to undergo sterilization procedures. If the couple do not appear, or if only one appears, there will be no birth certificate issued to the third child, but instead a third-child paper. The mother can be tattooed or marked to signify a third birth to any subsequent doctor. Instead of the missing parent, the child can be sterilized on the spot, insuring that this undue share of the gene pool will not be carried forward.

This is so distateful that extremely few parents would carry a third child past three months. Of these, even fewer would refuse sterilization after the third child is born. So it would be a rare child that was in fact sterilized under this scheme. If it were illegal to adopt native-born American children of living parents, there would be no selling of third children.

Such a scheme is totally different from the science-fiction pattern where human selection is carried out for the good of the race by "qualified" experts applying "scientific skills". In the first place there are no such qualified experts. In the second place, they could not help but select after themselves.

Fixing our present diversity as nearly as possible by permitting two children across the board to anyone who wants them is quite another approach. It has the great genetic advantage of protecting the diversity of our gene pools so that future demands for adaptation can be met from a wide range of capacities. There is no doubt that it is more in accord with our notions of fairness and intrinsic human rights to equal opportunity. Indeed, permitting two children to every couple continues that hazardous level of deselection we have already practiced on ourselves. But this is a lesser evil than the Pandora's box of positively selecting the progenitors of the future race. Those very groups who oppose voluntary controls, now, would be least likely to belong to the scientific ingroup enforcing genetic selection in a science-fiction future. They would be the losers in that kind of selection—and if they would, then so would all of us.

Thus, the urgency of population control runs: Stop at Two quickly; halt growth now. Enforce the limit of two for everyone when necessary, and defer as long as possible any system which attempts to choose among us for the progenitors of a new species. If we are so stupid as to let population explode to that point, most of us will prefer not to be there.

Status and Caste

19

PRESENT RATES of consumption are putting a very short time limit upon human tenure of the earth, if we look at the vanishing of oil, the polluting of the essential oceans, and the disappearance of trees. We are only tenants after all and it takes little to lose the ecological lease. That humans do not seem to care beyond the next generation, nor even very effectively for that, is something curious and terrible in us—a fatal lack in our species' equipment.

We will have used up in a mere handful of years, hardly more than a century, the accumulated petroleum reserves of ages. We go right on destroying with unctuous excuses the very balances which will give our descendants life. To the informed, this behavior seems monstrous, a folly so evil and discouraging that many of those most qualified to help feel hopeless.

Already, more times than we know of, humanity has had within it the seeds of its own rescue. Furthermore, despair is not the native attitude of men and women. We have understood our predicament only a short time, and that understanding has not yet spread widely among the ordinary people who carry out social change. When we leave doom-saying behind and begin the enterprise of rescue, behavior patterns will adapt to our new necessities. There is much to be expected from new efforts in America to develop population alternatives.

Although coercion may be the most effective way to control the population crisis, it is still the least accepted. Certainly if those groups who oppose all population programs were to team up with voluntary family planners to oppose the two-child limit, then only a few leaders would be urging measures severe enough to correct the problem before it is too late. Coercion has been an academic and not a legislative question because public opinion has only just begun to change. At least in America, the best way to change public opinion is to propose legislation and debate it widely. Once general public opinion favors reduction of population, then reduction will follow with a minimum of coercion. Meanwhile, the worse we allow the population problem to become the more drastic the remedy we will be forced to accept.

The political and emotional realities are complex. If we are to reduce the world's population by humane means we must recognize and reverse natalist pressures. In each social system we need to reverse current tendencies toward violence and repression, because genuine reduction in family size and total population will occur most easily in a framework of trust. In each religion, we need to identify the people and the ideas opposing population control, making clear that the need to reduce the number of births is not a religious question, but a matter of urgent scientific fact. The major task is to go out and get a consensus as quickly as possible.

A special problem confronts us here, because we are looking at a watershed, a true divide in human experience. The cohorts born before 1940 had no atom bomb hanging over their childhood; no TV assaulting their youth with violence, fear and sex; no draft taking the best years of their lives. They still remember an uncrowded, unmechanized world. They had experience of idealistic love and believable war.

The cohorts after 1946 have been progressively larger, crowded both from above and below. Now coming into adult years, they are speaking across a total gap in human experience to the adults who made it for them. The divide was not built by the young. They were not the overproducers of babies. They were not the architects of TV, or the A-bomb, or of space programs. They did not invent the credit card, the gross national product, nor the schemes to create full employment by planned obsolescence and planned waste. They did not measure prosperity by the weekly sale of cars, nor national progress in miles of new freeway. They were, and they still are, on the receiving end of all this.

The cohorts born between 1900 and 1930 are on the losing side of the divide. Small cohorts to begin with, often deeply opposed themselves to some of these events, they nevertheless now hold positions of concentrated power in economics, politics, medicine and education. They run the military. They run the press. Much of this power is entrenched to create, describe and defend a world that no one born after 1940 has any experience of. This watershed will move up the age structure of the population until soon no one under fifty will remember anything else but a violent, hungry and crowded world. This adds an urgency to solving the problem of ecology and population which no one likes to notice.

If we listen only to people already insensitive to crowding, indifferent to beauty, callous to living creatures and each other, then all we can expect from them is a diminished world.

Across this terrible divide between generations, filled with the extra anguish of civil and familial war, we must attempt the rescue of the ecosphere. But to do this may be possible only during the short time that living memory of a better world persists. The generations who took part in creating the impasse are also the only ones who recollect a dispersed America. Commanding most of the power to rebalance population with resources, they are glaring bemused into the generation gap, instead of rolling up their sleeves to rescue their own young flesh and blood. Much in the pages to follow can be remedied soon enough only by the post-reproductive cohorts. Tragically, too many of them are opposing the most necessary change in America; the wholehearted surrendering of ourselves to the task of controlling the human epidemic. The crisis in population is not only the fault of the breeding pair, but of factors built into society which encourage breeding.

The yellow-headed blackbird is a striking character from the marshes of northwestern America. The male deals in real estate. Dashing gold and black himself, his plain brown mates are much smaller. Like the medieval man, his notion of success is based on feudal boundaries from which he drives the intruder male with aggressive battle behavior. In the spring scramble for nesting sites, the odds are on the larger and maturer birds. The prize is waterfront property. Larger males obtain not the most square yards of marsh but the longest shoreline. Males with waterfronts attract more females into their territory and defend more nests and young than the males with small waterfronts. Careful ethological study of birds in the natural marsh reveals that during the raising of the young, the main food of these blackbirds is the abundant hatch of insects along the water's edge. Females seem to value real estate too. They accept sharing of the male in order to share in a productive property. In every nesting season the struggle for dominance is renewed.

Once the large blackbird male has won recognition of his territory, wives come to him without the need of aggression against them or against other males. The need for the male to prove himself in actual fighting subsides. He has won recognition of status. This has a peace-keeping, energy-conserving function.

There is an end result for the blackbirds. Hierarchy is established in the marsh. Peace follows. The qualities which gave a male breeding success will be selected for. The flashy male who can gain and keep a large territory will have more wives and may provide for more young during his seasons of vigor. But his defeated rivals will provide for young too. Thus the establishment of status is a protection for the blackbird population and a guarantee of selection for breeding success.

Both the status and the territory of the jaunty blackbird are curtailed if the population increases too rapidly, or if the area of the marsh is reduced. Competition for nesting sites and wives insures optimum spacing-out of the breeding units over the available range. There is an optimum balance between numbers of nests, insect hatches and long-term survival of the total ecosystem. So long as conditions which produce the leaders remain constant, the quality of the flock will be maintained because the dominant birds will have more offspring from more wives.

The dynamics of the Mormon family seem quite like the blackbird's, with multiple wives and separated nests. Both are essentially adaptations to holding large tracts of land. Like the blackbirds, Mormon leaders raised more offspring. The "monogamous" majority in America outlawed Mormon religious polygamy some years ago, although large families and opposition to birth control still characterize many Mormon communities. Whether the American majority was more upset by the frank intention to outbreed, or by the "immorality" of plural wives has never been made clear. It is clear, however, that the flourishing Mormon community has already survived a much greater inroad on their religious belief, and a much greater disruption of family pattern than the two-child limit would impose on the rest of us. This is a valid recent case where Americans intended to influence family size by enacting legislation.

While human society is more complex, less easily studied than the blackbirds in the marsh, the flashy plumage and the flashy car, the drive for real estate and for females are similar. In human society population increase has placed new pulls on all the old glue holding men in harmony. Personal importance and influence shrink with increasing density. Upward mobility depends on space in the ecosystem through which one can move. It also depends upon gaining attention which is easier in a smaller, more openly structured society.

Leadership in the wild and in simple human communities is usually due to inborn qualities of the individual: strength, speed, ferocity, cunning. In modern societies leadership is no longer only of this personal kind. Today, it may be rooted in social advantages. Leaders may be born into the nobility, or into the communist party or belong to a hereditary ruling caste of priests or warriors. The individual may have no ability and yet leadership may fall to him because of the position into which he was born.

No blackbird flashing across the marsh inherits his territory or his leadership. He has to scrap for it.

Generations of loons may "inherit" their fertile lake, or eagles inherit a valuable nesting crag. Perhaps herds inherit a home valley just as human groups inherit a range. But early man gives a new dimension to this word. Unlike our domestic animals he was aware of his kinship and descent throughout life. Awareness of descent and "inheritance" of things are linked together. Human inheritance quickly extended to knives, pots, skins, precious ancestor bones—and even more precious, to the transmitted tricks, father to son, of the hunting and fighting leaderships.

Early man could inherit things which gave him status, he could inherit secrets which gave him caste.

Status and caste differ in their effects on the population and on the child-bearing couple. Even though caste and status may exist side by side in complex societies as they do today in America, they differ in purpose and in emotional tone. Both systems organize people into patterns of obedience and leadership, both ultimately balance fighting with peace-keeping, both tend to channel and conserve the energies of the community in supporting itself. Status can be inherited to some degree, but must also be personally conserved. Self-made leaders cannot long survive the dwindling of their power, while the leader of a caste like a pope or a king may be very old, mad or senile. The reaction of these two types of leadership to population growth is quite distinct. Caste influence depends upon recruiting or producing members and the great castes of armies and priesthoods have been natalist forces throughout history. On the contrary, the great leaders of history with some notable exceptions have failed to found personal dynasties or to base their power on the fecundity of their followers.

Biology has a way of asserting itself in every political system. In spite of Marx no progress has been made in the withering away of governments. In the number of complex regulations and in the size of government Russia and the western democracies are running neck and neck. Bureaucracy is on a devouring rise. Lost on the happier side of the twentieth century mark is any notion that he who governs best would govern least. Density has been against it.

In a tight urban society the stress of status-seeking can be profoundly disturbing. Difference can be less irritating in rural communities where the buffer strips between families are larger. If my yard is half a mile down the road from your yard, I may love your flowers and you may admire my vegetables. We may even exchange. But if we are eight feet across a suburban driveway you not only rival my salary with your salary, but my lawn with your lawn, my children with your children. You feel that only clods raise vegetables and I feel only snobs raise flowers. Raw feelings develop over trivia. My bitch burns round spots in your grass; your dog burns brown limbs on my shrubbery. So we argue the bad points of dogs and bitches. Conformity to the block mores in grass, fence, curtains and porch furniture is extreme. Rare is the lawn with daisies, the house with a shack of boards, the rope swing with a muddy hole under it, the digging and delving of the unfettered human young. Rare is the old porch daybed with its lumpy pillow, or the dilapidated swinging couch where the young scuffed away hot afternoons to the soothing creak of its chains. Rare is the really comfortable shawl-laden armchair of the very old.

Sadly in America status-seeking has long since been divorced from any genuine function of peace-keeping, or energy-conserving, and has turned into a competitive conformity of the worst kind. This has led us to measure worth by such junk symbols as big cars, jewelry, publicity and yachts.

Suburban zoning codes in many cities require a set-back from the street, define hedge tops and proclaim a total lack of privacy and protection. Yet, inside a Spanish-type wall forbidden by the codes, I could grow my vegetables and you could grow your flowers and our dogs could snap at flies in peace. If we had a tattered chair or a shabby grandfather, he could doze in sun and sleep in shade, forgetting to button his clothes with tranquillity.

As density moves in on us, as we live closer and compete harder, buffer zones, silence, variety and privacy become ever more necessary but ever more the privilege of the rich. We can destroy difference; we can down-grade privacy. But the real problem is to restore optimum levels of density, and to be single-minded about it. In city design, in architecture of apartments and housing projects, we need new imaginations of harmony.

The human spirit belongs to us all and steps to nourish it are as important as steps toward providing jobs and food. Dense living conditions do not abolish the need to escape, the need to mingle, the need for beauty, the need for decent essentials.

Above all, density intensifies the need for the family "heartland". "A man's house is his castle" expresses a primitive truth for territory-defending primates. But this central womb of necessarily safe territory has become a transient's flat no more lasting that the night-nest of a wandering gorilla. Instead of fixing a family into the neighborhood structure and raising children with duties and roots, the welfare authorities in America move people up and down according to payments and family size. The notion of neighborhood, which is biological and fosters security in the young and the old, has been lost along the way. Yet all over the world, ownership of even the littlest piece of land is clung to with a desperate dignity. People hunger for true neighbors. This need will not be abolished. It is more humane, much more practical to reduce density, the recent intruder!

If we were to turn our ideas upside down, and to attack inner-city problems, poverty problems from the biological view, we would not contemplate compendious buildings. We would revive neighborhoods. We would attempt to measure how big is big, how much is enough. We would cut births and distribute the breeding population more evenly over available space. But dispersion of people also has biologic limits. The need for a food base under urban populations conflicts with suburban sprawl. The psychic need for green space close-in conflicts with density. The ratio of cost to benefit worsens rapidly as these invisible balance points are overstepped.

We can make our cities important and exciting places to live. We can make them healthy places to live, but not at the same time that we funnel the nation's poor into them from everywhere else. We can expand public education and housing and sanitation, but not at the same time that city wages rise and taxes shrink. Condensed poverty, like any other condensed center of disease cannot be lived with. It must be cleaned out. Everybody cries for improvement, but nobody wants to sacrifice personal status to pay for it. Unions resist sacrificing the minimum wage. We realize suddenly, that those laws so long fought for now abolish the first rung of the job ladder for American youngsters beginning to work. Teachers will not sacrifice the hard-won tenure system which strangles school curriculum and prevents vital personnel change. Owners cling to old zoning and building codes. Thousands of people in government want status protected for them by social contracts and licenses. They want guaranteed employment. But this *is* radical change in the flux of American life! Security strikes at upward mobility, at the universal hopes of the young. With crowding, demand for status protection can lead to an ever-more closed and irritable society. It is against this closing off of opportunity that outbreaks are taking place.

In American society, status-seeking has fed competition, upward mobility and the great producing, consuming juggernaut of industrial prosperity of the sixties. Overall, it has been good. Our status society keeps within itself the possibility of a more open society in the future. Nevertheless, unemployment is a major illness. Poverty is a prison. We have not solved these in the midst of prosperity. When we compare our poor to the poor of other lands, we should feel encouraged. When we compare our poor to the average in America, we should be not only ashamed but baffled.

Cruel as it often is, a status society has one great advantage. It has no stake in increasing its population.

The small family is compatible with prominence, and so is the small nation. We look with pride upon Switzerland and Sweden, upon Finland which defended itself so royally and paid off its debts, to modern Canada and recent Japan. These nations are respected for their powerful place in science and humanities, for their improved conditions at home and their improved relations abroad.

Political stability and civil progress are adversely affected by crowding. The most populous and the most rapidly breeding nations are not admired. Overbreeding elicits pity, fear and contempt for nations as well as families.

In India, one of my hosts made the casual and not entirely serious remark that Australia which was "empty", should take a hundred million Indians. This was a particularly humane, scholarly man, and though he was jesting I vividly remember my reaction of sympathy and yet shock and disbelief. One can agree when he speaks of "empty" Australia. But why should Australia take Indians? Undisciplined breeding has ruined the land of India, and is a totally undesirable export. One must admit this, no matter how much one likes India or enjoys her people. Thirteen million live in Australia now. India's *increase per year* is thirteen million. The contrast shocks. There is something wrong here, dangerous to overlook, perhaps deadly.

What the Japanese did with abortion, India could do. What the Kalahari bushmen can do with self-discipline, India has claimed she can do. But the drive to breed is everywhere in India—pervasive—built into the temples of the past and the mores of the present. The breeding pair in India behaves like an invading army populating in order to hold onto the land. For centuries, they did exactly this. Indians are being excluded from other countries in a purely tribal reaction to this unchecked fecundity. Once the Indian breeding pair makes the transition from caste to status and stops at two, they may be welcomed into other countries as citizens. But not before. Sensitive, impulse-ridden India blames Australians for a color bar. But color is the lesser part of the story. Black Africa dispossessed Indian merchants not because of color, but in fear of being commercially dominated through their caste system by this intelligent, fecund people.

No effort at national production in India could approach the per-capita impact on living standards of a total halt in reproduction. When India's Minister of Family Planning, Sripati Chandrasekhar suggested just this to the Lokh Sabha in honor of Gandhi's centennial year, he was far from joking. The breeding pair in India is the problem and so far no one has found the key. But the caste system may be the tangle in which it lies hidden; intense personal pride of race and caste.

For two thousand years the same scene was repeated: invasions, military adventures and rises and falls of power. Many different tribes ruled India in turn. Under new conquerors, the beaten owners of rich valleys became cultivator castes. In time, after several of these inflows, the lower castes looked quite different from the rulers, had different religious beliefs, languages, marriage customs, and food taboos. Embedded in some of the lowest caste practices are the cultural patterns of the earliest ruling Indus and Ganges people. They are ethnic fossils preserved by the caste system, and vastly fascinating therefore.

Survival of the conquered was protected by caste. Subjection was assured. Very astute!

There is no equality in India. But until recently there has been a security in relations between castes which lent great flexibility and toughness to the civilization. Caste endured as a system for absorbing conquest. Change and invasion were recognized simply by adding new castes as required. It was no fault of the individual if he was born lower or higher, dark or light. Each could attain perfection by perfecting his life in its appointed niche. Acceptance of caste led to a static noncompetitive society. It was a fascinating solution to the need for harmony in diversity, for tolerance after conflict.

Indian castes may be the closest approximation human societies have yet made to the pattern of breeding exclusion shown by bird species who share a common territory. Caste in its extreme form in India provides separate walks of life, separate trades, foods, religions and dwelling places for exclusive marriage circles. Except that castes are cross-fertile and some illicit gene-flow persisted, the separation into noncompeting niches was nearly as complete in 1850 as it is now for birds. To the western mind, such a caste system seems a total inversion of ethical values. But as a peace-keeping pattern assigning a role to everyone, it succeeded for many hundreds of years, until the advent of death control and the pressures of density, and industrialization.

There is latent, however, in the caste form of society a vested interest in births and clan increase. Fertility is worshipped. Sons are wanted. Having many children has been important not just to the mother and father but to the marriage circle and wider caste kinships as well. Within the caste framework, individual importance may depend upon the number of male kin, brothers, uncles, sons, and nephews a man can mobilize.

Any attempt to limit population in a caste society runs up against this need for offspring which has been economic, political and religious. Still unresolved in modern India are conflicts between caste loyalty and the increasing cost to the kinship and to the country, of the enlarging family.

Western eagerness to reject the Hindu caste system as undemocratic and backward should be tempered by a look at its strong points. Diversity of artistic and religious life, of character and dress make India one of the most decorative and complex societies in the world. The system at its best provided physical and psychic security for rich and poor. The commercial system now encroaching upon it has yet to do so. But the natalist component of caste needs to be isolated and its remedies defined.

This is the more critical as a research project when we come back to the scene in America. For here we have a simplification of caste, its exacerbation in modern society, and the effects of its inherent natalism.

In the United States, the American Negro, the American Indian, and the Mexican-American form three rather distinct originally rural castes as a consequence of the European conquest of the continent. Among these peoples, marriage circles rarely overlap; gene-flow is reduced. The anomaly of caste in a supposedly democratic society can only be understood if we recognize its separation of victor from vanquished and its peace-keeping character.

Disenfranchising the freed slaves was a caste solution. Indian reservations were a caste solution. White apartheid, black solidarity are caste solutions. None of them meet the need of modern technical society.

The changeover from caste to status underlies racial unrest in America today. This transfer has hardships of a special kind. We do not know how to do it. Hurtful attitudes and behavior are scarring the transition. Older warm relations are gone. New ones are slow in coming.

Caste in modern voting societies is a breeding problem. The white south used every means to control the vote; now urban blacks are using their votes to elect city officials and to rearrange urban priorities. Both white and black are conscious of breeding as a road to voting power. At a time when urban industrial society as a whole experiences a declining birth rate, the urban black rate is not declining and militants do not intend it to.

One-man, one-vote works so long as there is no language, religious, or physical difference to perpetuate. But when the American colonies expanded and took in different peoples, breeding isolates developed, fear of majority rule arose, and produced the gut reaction—to breed. We need a new solution to the caste problem in voting societies, which will protect the ethnic integrity and habits of minorities. Each one of us ought to respond to this quest, for each of us is a lonely minority of one. We can gauge how dangerous this loneliness can be if we recall that the partition of India from Pakistan was brought about by the one-man, one-vote formula of the Congress party government. Six million Hindus and Moslems were killed in the shuffle—who had been neighbors and had spoken the same languages for three hundred years. It happened far away in India, where to most ordinary Americans six million more or less seems unreal. But we ought to take that tribal outbreak seriously, because it could happen here.

We are terribly primitive, terribly unprepared to sort out these complex disorders. As a nation, as biologists and social scientists, we have not really looked with detachment and care into the task of fusing castes into a single society. Caste is not merely a bias against the dark-skinned peoples, but also is a mechanism for perpetuating cherished and possibly very valuable differences. We do not really know whether castes can disappear into a biologically stable system. We do not know whether they ought to.

We do know that emancipation, the vote, education are status solutions. Opportunity in business and professions and private organizations are status solutions. When political systems move away from caste and military control toward status solutions, population can drop, other values can enter the arena. Then allegiance to likeness, to brotherhood may become a species solution. The open society may be born.

In one more vital respect, caste and status differ. Caste has a body language. Most children caught unawares by a foreigner cower as the young gulls cower before an intruder. We react to visible racial difference as a gull or a crow reacts, and we learn this before word-language by copying the body-language of adults. Ritual caste greetings were peace signs. Caste survival required such rituals in the past. Continuing survival of human racial difference may require them in the future. We must study human behavior systems, biologically and genetically, for once we let our difference seem more important than our likeness, we might close up our gene pools and attempt to outbreed each other. This would be the greatest threat to human stability. It would be a dismal joke if deliberate social isolation were to bring about the speciation which geographic isolation failed to accomplish. If we are to remain one species, tribal and caste difference, color, language and religion will have to blur their edges before our common future, whether we like it or not. Of all arguments for reducing caste barriers, this is the most biological, the most human. The open society calls us. But into its promise of equality must also go the ritual distance, the formal courtesy which tempers friction and protects our differences.

The Open Society

20

TRADITIONAL SOCIETIES in many parts of the world are like the blackbirds of the marsh. Mere animal fertility has been the badge of success. In Latin America having a large number of children is the only status open to most poor males. "Machismo" for the male requires that his virility be recognized by himself and others, but this occurs only as the numbers of his children increase. Entrapped in old village or new barrio, there is no opening out of social circles where his other male abilities can become valuable.

Until fifty years ago, these countries had a death rate high enough to keep up with the birth rate. The male came of age only after the birth of a son. To get a son, he often sired a lot more children than he needed. Thoughtless removal of death controls from this population has had a catastrophic result on growth. Births have soared beyond the capacity of public programs to deal with them. American aid triggered the problem in the first place with medical help and death control. But resentment toward the United States and continuing Catholic opposition restricts aid in birth control. Growth rates of 3%, doubling times of twenty-three years are not uncommon south of the border. Poverty is not decreasing. Today there are neither jobs nor emigration to absorb the influx of young workers at the bottom of the heap. Yet lack of other values keeps the birth rate high. An internal crash is probable and it may bring worldwide disaster along with it.

Sudden increase in density in primarily rural peoples has thus aggravated the old-standing cruelty of a closed society. Offering contraception alone will not succeed. Approval of the large family must be turned into public and *Catholic* disapproval. The Catholic Church can do only one humane thing in this decade—approve the small family norm!

So far, most changes of government in South America have made little dent upon the closed society. Growth of free associations has been slow. Education is low. The army, dominated by the ruling class, overshadows everything. To dent Latin fertility patterns it will be necessary to open out other forms of satisfaction to men and women, and to offer other kinds of recognition and reward.

In the open society, each person lives in many overlapping circles of interest and activity. Finding importance and self-value in one of them is not too difficult. Flower shows, sky-diving, fishing derbies, Little League, mushroom societies, hill-climbs and organized charities are strange zoological behaviors, but sound for social health. With expansion of the arts and professions, personalities are enriched. If value can be centered on the quality of community life, and on the free input of individual efforts, neither large families nor large groups will be needed for security. In the open society an outright drop in population can be an advantage.

American life still offers unexpected chance for recognition; there are many rewards which do not come even indirectly from government, even though commercial life is full of hierarchy and harsh competition. Cruel as it is, our society is beginning to recognize its stake in abolishing poverty. The flaw in the American dream today lies in the people it excludes from the system; the old, the poor, the ethnic minorities; and its young people. An open society can flourish best when the whole population is included. There must be status satisfactions for everyone, many links in the chains of authority, and much slack in the links. Schools and universities are not branches of government in the open society, and are not kept in order by the police or the army. Money talks, but it flows into such multiple channels that it has an invigorating effect over a total landscape of possible human activity. Necessary social change can arise rapidly because institutions and techniques already exist, upon which new forms can be modeled. Fortunately social change occurs this way in many countries.

In the open society, neither sexual warfare, nor military adventure is necessary to the expression of human aggression. All kinds of physical, artistic and commercial aggressions can be expressed, where there is freedom to choose trades and avocations, and to become acquainted early with the realities of choosing.

The ideal open society offers a model for the future. It buffers one group from another by offering them different social options, but identical legal remedies. It is an egalitarian, secular, opportunistic society, sure enough of itself to permit strong identity and exclusion patterns. It offers more advantages and fewer drawbacks to the small group and the small family than either caste or status systems. Open societies have had kings, oligarchs, and parliaments. They are not necessarily democratic, and have resulted only rarely from revolution.

One hallmark of an open society is the flourishing of institutions that are neither political nor religious. Like the guilds of the Middle Ages, modern organizations serve to isolate yet support their members. Exclusive marriage circles can survive without imposing penalties for marrying-out. Status differences emerge, but without roots in hereditary privilege. Hereditary power can survive in dynasties like Hearst and Beaverbrook, Rockefeller and duPont, but without ruling position. Religions can survive but without government support. When all these forces together are in dynamic counterpoise, they impose a general restraint upon each other and upon the powers of government. The ideal society and the life styles it fosters offer a measure of the quality of life in communist, capitalist and junta countries.

Against the concept of the open society, all forms of modern government can be found wanting, and toward it all forms of government can be encouraged to modify.

In Anglo-Saxon countries the flourishing of organizations has been carried to extremes. The clubwoman, the gregarious male joiner are humorous figures. But their very absurdity is vastly important. For they are the opposite of fertility figures! They represent a new dimension of the human potential. They stand for nonreproductive group activity directed to social ends.

Nothing is so precious to evolving social possibility and nothing is so easily destroyed as these multifarious, anarchic and opposing private organizations. Except for full-time, coerced employment of women nothing offers so genuine an alternative to overbreeding. It may prove very unwise to hinge population reduction on the full-time employment of women in a world where jobs are scarce and people plentiful.

Today we tend to think only of politics, protest and imprisonment when we think of free association. But it has a much larger, more luminous horizon than that. If we think back to the Greek societies, to the guilds of Florence and London, to the original universities and the modern foundation, it is easier to understand "free associations". Today they offer an unhampered arena for good ideas and bubbling enterprise, where men and women associate to produce all kinds of human change. They are continuing "rap sessions" organized for concerted action.

The overpowering federalization of America threatens these free organizations and the open society. Despotism through non-response is as deadly in effect as despotism through directive. We cannot stop highways, pipelines, poison gas, DDT, dams or population because THEY aren't listening. And if organizations like the Sierra Club or the public foundations make enough noise to be heard, the Internal Revenue Service moves in on them. The power to tax is the power to destroy, and in the name of protecting society, the free-spoken, independent organizations and individuals are being muzzled.

The internal enemy of the open society is over-regulation. The external is communal friction. When polarization of communal factions threatens the open society, then stepped-up governmental regulation threatens it too.

Among nations, we also need an open society instead of military alliances, for today the price and problems are changing. Nations as well as individuals have been status seekers and defenders of territory. Now atomic weapons have upset the old patterns. Only those nations which buttress the heartland by defensive arms, yet threaten no other territory can expect to live in peace and safety. We are too primitive a world for total disarmament, and too technical a world for major war. Fragmentation on the basis of language and race is taking place around the world. Tensions run high. Yet history doubtless will record the trilingual Swiss, the bilingual Belgians as successful federations. A bilingual Quebec, Province of Canada, has more future than an isolated French State of Quebec. A United States of America has been more viable for north and south than separated states would have been. Even more crucial, the overall harmony of the continent and the exchange of its resources has been well served by unity. We are free of borders and customs duties, and restrictions upon citizenship. We are free of military checkpoints. An American with a driver's license can transact business anywhere within the largest customs union in the world. We forget how costly this was to win and how much other parts of the world have struggled for similar unification in trade. For centuries, the imperialists in Europe and Asia sought unification of territory for peace-keeping reasons. The United States of Europe—for so long the dream of later Federalists—may be realized at last for reasons of technology. But to the citizen of the enlarged states, the real advantage will lie in a more varied, opportunistic society in which it will not be advantageous to overbreed.

The United Nations gives expression to a priority which is new: species self-interest, although tribal self-interests are still effectively tearing it apart. Unfortunately the tendency of the last decades has been to fragment along tribal lines. Jomo Kenyatta survived English imprisonment to become the leader of his Kikuyu tribesmen in the new government of Kenya. His counterpart, in the government from the Luau tribe was Tom Mboya, equally patriotic, intelligent, British-educated, yet the Kikuyu killed Mboya in their tribal struggle for power, rending Kenya. One-man, one-vote has been accepted by the new nations without any scientific doubts at all. The United Nations have not looked the biological problem of tribal survival in the face. Ideology has interfered. Yet after Biafra, after the death of Tom Mboya, we ought to doubt; we need to inquire. Anglo-Saxons have to go no further than Belfast to discover that a "tribe" has to feel secure as a legal and political entity independent of numbers. Viability cannot be reckoned by nose-counting. Votes alone will not secure the future. If population reduction is to succeed, the small tribe vis-à-vis the large one must feel it can exist. The nations leading the world's educational and technical development have never led in the population race. They are drastically outnumbered, and the prospects are that they will be even more so before the developing countries can steady down to zero growth. Surely the answer is not a sudden burst of breeding which tries to erase the advances of the last three hundred years! Surely it lies in models of harmony, in happier patterns of existing life.

Conflict can be deliberately fostered or deliberately reduced by our own behavior. We need to reduce conflicts which encourage breeding reactions. We need models of harmony, imaginations of sharing. Human populations have filled the earth for less than three centuries. They have really feared crowding for less than fifty years. It is too soon to expect adaptations to have emerged among us. Bird populations have been filling up niches around the world for much longer than this. Birds have many more generations per century than any human tribe, and among them new patterns have emerged. The swallows of the hill farm offer one of them. On the hill farms of America are some acres of hay, or mountain grain. Old pastures surround the pioneer barn. On the sagging roof, multicolored with lichens, the swallows congregate. The violet-greens build in special crevices tucked back along the old beams. The barn swallow builds a mud saucer applied to the open sides of rafters. Under the eaves on the outside of the barn are the clay jugs of the cliff swallow.

In spring, these swallows gather eagerly at the edge of a puddle. With their beaks full of mud they swoop on the wing for the barn. At the nest they flutter in place, and with jabs of bill add to their careful masonry. Certain ruts in the cart tracks provide just the right wet clay, springtime after springtime.

From each type of nest the young swallow must take off on the wing without a single practice flight. He must lean over the edge, gaze into the natural medium of air, and fly. Expert, dexterous, fast and erratic, these masters of flight get along without apparent conflict. They do not quarrel for nesting sites between species. Each chooses near but quite different real estate. One barn swallow may dispute a choice beam with his own kind. All of them may suddenly compete in aerobatics for a flying chicken feather, the victor flying off to "feather" his nest. They do not interfere with each other in the hunt for food. There is more than enough food in the insect hatches for all of them. The three species do not usually hawk insects at the same altitudes nor over the same terrain. But all of them can be seen crisscrossing each others' flight paths and sailing through each others' hunting altitudes. All of them share the evening hatches above the pond. As the young are fledged, they gather along the old wires leading from barn to house. Later they move to multiple wires along the road where small flocks from many farms begin to mingle. The songs, the circlings, the splashes into and out of pond and the quick twitters are so much a part of the hill farm that one rarely stops to notice. Yet here, amid the most competitive, exacting task of the year, amid the hatching and raising of the young, there is harmony.

What makes this possible?

There must be certain buffers in the system. There is obvious social pleasure of flying and feasting and bathing. We too, respond to festivals of flying and feasting and bathing. Although the swallows are closely related species of the same genus, unlike human tribals, they never interbreed. There is no sexual aggression among them. Swallows never increase to an infestation and they have yet to disappear altogether. The ecosystem harvests them; they do not have to harvest each other. Therefore, their harmony is never tested because numerous as they may seem to us against the August sky, they never experience crowding.

Warblers also at first glance appear to disobey the classical rule of separate niches. These are small butterfly birds many of which forage daily in mixed flocks through the northern evergreens. By placing trained observers at specific trees, by making accurate counts of insects taken, and by later stomach counts, Robert H. MacArthur (1958) documented that certain of these species travel together, and live in the same evergreens, but are NOT living on the same food nor occupying the same niche. Far from it! Different insects abound at different places on the fir. The traveling bands of warblers divide up the fir by geography of high and low, by trunk, branch and tip, and thus specialize on different kinds of insects. Rather than competing for the same food, they carefully exploit all the different food niches on the tree—much as the caste system exploits all the different livelihoods in a village in India.

MacArthur's study corroborates that where these species coexist, niches are separate. Neither food nor living space is an issue among them. Where races of men coexist in harmony, we surmise food and living space are not at issue. If two very different peoples have arrived in the same valley and both expect to live on the same food and water supply and to occupy the same space, they have two choices, battle or merger. Too often in human history the outcome has been battle first and then merger of the remnants! Today, all over the world, battle, merger, and peaceful coexistence are going on at the same time.

American pioneer families spaced out to hold the land, and used their high breeding potential. Long after patterns of spacing-out ceased to be possible, the large family and high birth rate persisted as part of the American past. But high offspring number combined with high density of pairs is unstable. Today, the large family could persist successfully only if total human numbers were steeply reduced.

Modern urban humans tend rather to follow the opposite direction accepting close living conditions by sharply reducing offspring per pair. It is a rookery bird from New York who says to the spaced-out bird from Kansas, "Gee, this place is empty. It can take lots more people!" The Kansas bird replies just as truthfully, "You don't know how full it is!" Both are correct. Only because Kansas is "empty" and productive, the urban crowds in New York can be fed.

The passenger pigeon reminds us there is no safety in large numbers either. The pigeon flew in greater flocks than recorded for any other bird in North America. Its favorite food was the beech mast of the Appalachian forests. It wandered far and wide in enormous hungry flights, foraging west through the prairie groves of the central states, north to the edge of the firs and hemlocks, and south into the dense mixed hardwoods of the southern mountains. Man cleared the woods, and shot the pigeon. One wonders if the extent of the forest-felling, or the degree of slaughter was recognized at the time by anyone taking part in it. The pigeon's enormous numbers were offset by lowered breeding. It paired for life. In the sudden pressure, surviving birds could not make up for birds killed, and widowed birds refusing to mate again. From natural disaster many species recover in time but from man, the market-hunter and feller of forests, the pigeon could not recover. Huge numbers offered them no final protection. No wonder as we think of dying-off, our minds are drawn to harmony, to the swallows of the hill farm, the warblers of the fir.

Americus, through accident and illusion, has opposed constructing boundaries in North America. We are an evolutionary experiment in the large territory, the free migration of tribals, the loose common language. Irrelevant in this huge expanse, where you come from, what foods you like, what gods you worship! But not yet irrelevant the color of skin, the slant of eye, though this too, is on the species agenda. Perhaps never again will such a chance come, in conditions so hopeful. . . .

Civilized brotherhood rests lightly over our ancient unrest, because millions of years of evolutionary wisdom have made us uneasy with visible difference. Throughout biology, visible difference has been the key to speciation, to separation of peoples. Therefore, blacks and whites living as Americans have the civilized dream in their keeping. They guard the cradle of possibility. They are watchers in the night around the same campfire. Already languages, religions and fiercely opposed nationalities have subsided at this campfire, have protected this cradle. Species Americus offered a civilized dream to Nordic and Mediterranean, Irish and Pole, all visibly different. Now the issue is fairly joined. These people are of us, among us, not over some sea. They belong to the dream. They are the test of it. Hopefully this turmoil of race relations is the final struggle of tribalism against the species potential.

These great moments when the direction of species life is about to change forever are charged with danger to all selfish and unseeing animals. The ecosystem redirects them. A Zen Satori overcomes them; a mystic view transforms them. New patterns run from sleep and dreams into daytime behavior. The busy lives of the world move in new directions without registering the change. So the great shift from the tribal to the species life, the shift from breeding to sharing may have to come from the ecosystem, from the happening of the festival, because we are not yet wise enough to design it nor harsh enough to enforce it ourselves.

When fire came to the human tribe, the hearth came and women became hearth-keepers. The protection offered by the hearth entrapped us, even though we continued to roam.

Once a woman allows the specter of too many births to haunt her, to touch her nerve endings, she will recognize the protection of the small family. Like responding to the warmth of fire on the living flesh, the sexual and emotional flesh will respond to a new wanting. Change will come over the tribal patterns. The reply of the flesh to the needs of human survival will create a natural population control.

Natural and Unnatural

21

IN WESTERN COUNTRIES descended from the Roman empire, what is unnatural not only has its original overtones of magic, but its Christian overtones of sinfulness. In Faust and in many another western tale, the unnatural is wicked, and the natural is good. So long as many people believe it is natural to have children and unnatural to prevent them, the necessary about-face on family size will not occur. Many religions have taught deliberately that the large family is natural. We need to realize that in different circumstances, the small family is natural too.

Because population reduction is a basic condition for many other improvements, idealistic people will devote themselves to it, and will pour into it the moral energies needed for social change when it seems both natural and right. If there is a population crisis, but abortion and sterilization are not the moral ways to deal with it, is contraception? If contraception is not moral either, will abstinence do the job? The answer to this has been a resounding *no* from all quarters. Such an impasse between need and morality forces us to question the context in which such moral judgments came to be made. When reason tells us that population must reduce, and only by reducing births will this occur humanely, then reason also tells us that to reduce births must be natural and right.

Whenever religion places itself in contradiction to reason, it places itself also in contradiction to the moral sense. Only with the sense of truth coexists the sense of the right and good.

(Ludwig Feuerbach, *The Essence of Christianity*, Chapter 25, p. 246.)

The peculiar power of the words natural and unnatural over the uneducated peoples of the West comes from the religious history of these words. What we think natural to do is bound up with the notion of a natural law. Natural law comes to us from the roots of Mediterranean civilization, from the times when the deserts of Asia Minor were still hanging green gardens and rivers of delight. The early Judaic obsession with laws, begetting, fornication and sexual acts contrary to nature is understandable if we remember the context of a pastoral, herding people. Sodomy is still common on farms today. Inbreeding of livestock is practiced by most herdsmen. The effort to distinguish between what is right for an animal and what is not right for a human was an absorbing task for these early societies. The notion of natural and unnatural acts took root here. The British legal heritage upon which American common law is based runs back through Rome to Greece and Asia Minor, but in Rome the legalistic framework was begun. Slave-owning Roman society falls far short of modern political ideals, but at that time equality of free men before Roman law was an extraordinary departure from tribal modes of thought. Equality before the law became a powerful unifying force within the empire, applying to foreigners with strange languages and religions in the Pax Romana. Tribes were attracted into the empire by its promise of peace, by its equal protections and its expansions of trade. This was the first political notion of a law applying equally to many types of men. Roman law carried the stamp of this early internationalism far into the turbulent scenes of later Europe.

In their effort to escape from the narrow exclusiveness of tribal life, the early Christian fathers took the pattern of the

Roman empire over into the early Roman church. The germ of an international supervening sacred law was born. This became a weapon in their battle against local paganism and feudalism. The early Christian fathers were then able to argue that local law not in accord with natural law was void. For St. Augustine, disobedience to courts and kings mattered little so there was obedience to God. Within this sacred "natural law" the early church forbade witchcraft and magic, and sexual acts "against nature". Acts against nature remain prohibited in the Roman church. In the rest of society definitions of what those acts are have been modified by changing times. In particular, sexual behavior of consenting adults has been shifting to the area of privacy.

St. Thomas held that a rational, divine order of goodness and justice was placed over both man and God. Man, by God's grace could obtain it. But such a dual position provoked the spark of later revolts. For if man by his share in the divine reason could judge whether the law be just and good, he could also judge the laws of the church and the behavior of prelates. He could follow his reason to protest against unjust law, and lastly he could defy it.

The *Summa Theologiae* of St. Thomas largely rules the Roman church today. It led directly to the breaking away of the Protestant conscience from control by Rome and to revolts of the governed against the unrestricted powers of kings. Reason escaped from the divines in the Reformation and was declared by Martin Luther to belong to common men who must consult it to guide their conscience. Escaping from the church, reason then blazed out in disobedience to courts and kings. In the final outbreak against the corrupt Bourbon kings, the torch of reason was plunged into the powder keg of revolutionary France. The gentle light of reason of the middle ages became the bloody Goddess of Reason of the French Revolution. Today reason is again embattled on the side of humane population control.

The Greek definition of man as the rational animal expresses what we feel about ourselves. We dread the future, plan action and expect events in a way different from all other animals. St. Thomas says, "Natural law is nothing else than the rational creature's participation in the eternal law" (*Summa Theologiae*, "On the Various Kinds of Law," p. 618, Question XCI Q.91, a.2).

Aquinas' second question on natural law asked if the precepts are one or many. He replies, "The first precept of law: that good is to be done and promoted, and evil is to be avoided. All other precepts of the natural law are based on this" (ibid., "The Natural Law," p. 637, Question XCIV Q.94, a.2).

Aquinas lists three orders of natural inclinations in man. They have a proverb-like familiarity. First of all, ". . . every substance seeks preservation of its own being and by reason of this inclination whatever is a means of preserving human life and of warding off its obstacles belongs to the natural law" (ibid.). (Fire seeks to blaze, water returns to water, life seeks to stay alive.)

Secondly, "Those things are said to belong to the natural law which nature has taught to all animals, such as sexual intercourse, the education of offspring and so forth" (ibid.).

Thirdly, ". . . man has an inclination to good according to the nature of his reason, which nature is proper to him. Thus man has a natural inclination to know the truth about God and to live in society—whatever pertains to this inclination belongs to the natural law—to shun ignorance, to avoid offending those among whom one has to live" (ibid., p. 638). All of these precepts of the law of nature have the character of one natural law inasmuch as they flow from one first precept: to pursue good and avoid evil.

Aquinas points out that natural law is the same for all men but not equally known by them. Then he reasserts our peculiar western heritage in unmistakable terms: ". . . just as in man reason rules and commands the other powers, so all the natural inclinations belonging to the other powers must need be directed according to reason. Therefore it is universally right for all men that their inclinations should be directed according to reason" (ibid., p. 642, Q. 94, a.4).

The protestant conscience appeals to the supremacy of the first principle—to promote good and avoid evil, and to the last precept—that in man reason rules, to arrive at a flexible and adaptive idea of what natural law requires of man as an animal. Today the pressure of population threatens preservation of species life, so that now many Christians believe birth control is natural under the first precept, survival. Furthering species survival certainly falls under the rule of what is natural to human behavior. Thus we not only need to feel that birth control, abortion and sterilization are natural responses, but we need to approve them.

Catholic objections to modern divorce, to homosexuality, contraception and abortion stem from an inflexible attitude toward the second precept, those things which *nature has taught to all animals*. Nature does not teach birth control, but nature enforces population control on all animals, except on temporary modern man. Division of opinion in the Catholic church today flows from conflict between concern for the survival of man, and the need for survival of the intact dogma of the church. Throughout two thousand years, the humanistic, rational control of the church has been impressive. It has opposed barbarism and rebuked power, and adapted dogma to need. Today the church is again in process of adapting natural law to the new necessities of mankind. When the next pope conforms the past to the future, birth control and the small family will cease to be an issue dividing congregations.

The revolutionary theory of natural rights arose from natural law. Individual conscience and the equality of man blazed out in the American and French revolutions, and turned natural right into modern civil liberties.

Natural law also led straight to the western theory of science. From natural law accessible to reason, Roger Bacon thought we could deduce the rational sequence of events in physical nature. Though this turned out to be mistaken, his fame and his rationalism gave a new direction to medieval thought.

In the same century, William of Occam was a scholastic in the more empirical tradition of Aquinas. Occam developed Aquinas' notion that similar events have similar causes, but he came to the sweeping new idea that one natural cause was sufficient to a natural event. Magic did not intervene. Divinity need not be looked to for explanations in nature. Practical inquiry was enough to reveal the natural cause—and within the domain of practical life there was no unnatural cause. God never interfered capriciously in the physical world. This was the scholastic's vision of a divinely rational world and orderly nature. It was a remarkable vision, a powerful and effective tool in questioning and controlling physical events. On such a premise science could proceed to develop its later models of inquiry, experiment and comparison. The empirical tradition of western science laid magic to rest. Reason and nature were able to escape from superstition and explore the facts.

Even today, although we talk in science of regularities rather than causes, our joy in symmetry, in coherence, in logical power and definitive experiment is still more than an intellectual exercise. It retains something of the sweep and poignance of those early observers, discovering anew the order of reason in nature and in man.

Within this period, the church many times opposed new discoveries as heresies, and burned heretics at the stake for their opinions. It took ninety years for the excommunication against Galileo to be reversed by the church. The fact is that it was reversed. Today, no one believes the sun revolves around the earth. Furthermore, and this is the most important point— no one believes that the church has any *jurisdiction* on the question. Whatever the spiritual value offered by the church to the believer, how the sun revolves is not a part of it. But in saying this, we are looking back upon a conflict which was deep and bitter and carried to extremes, before the church lost out to the forces of that reason it had done so much to encourage.

Finally, between the 16th and the 19th century, science broke from miracles and religion altogether and came onto an independent foundation.

In the last century, the church set itself against the evidence for evolution. Science and reason and the evidence of the rocks won again. Whatever was left of the notion of a personal creation was pushed by extensions of physical science into the much further distance. Similarly the modern church has doubtful jurisdiction over the scientific question of population control.

From the farthest stars to the deepest oceans we hunt our answers today not in chapel and sacred precincts but in observatories and laboratories and field experiment. We are forced by the uncompromising seriousness of science to replace new fact in old fabrics, to pursue truth at the expense of dogma, to write down as failures those beliefs which conflict with the basic tenets of our science.

For two centuries at least, success in science has led to practical developments which have altered our lives beyond recognition. We did not foresee what would happen to society as a result of basic inventions, and the technology which burgeoned from them. Benefits to the quality of general human life have been so spectacular that the process of scientific invention has become a sort of public property. Generations of people are alive today who have watched the hiring of scientists to do certain jobs: to go to the moon, to sail under the north pole ice, to set up a communications satellite, to find the measles and polio vaccines, to destroy malaria. This attitude of hire toward science even threatens its ultimate future, for science is not in the contracting business. Its business is discovery, experimentation, and criticism of results. To range freely over the landscape without being told what to produce is one of the essential needs of young scientists. Inquiry for its own sake must be supported. Interference by ideology or racial bias is destructive. Science ought not to become a branch of the body politic. Only in knowledge for its own sake is there any guarantee of an ultimately honest opinion, an ultimately honest seeing. It is too easy to impose small notions of good and evil on the larger patterns of events. Better that science go unsupported than become the lackey of any church, political system, or military complex.

Individual scientists have been grant- and power-hungry, and have lost sight of their roots in the humanistic tradition. They have used their prestige in science to promote their local, ordinary opinions. Experts are testifying for and against everything from birth control and oil spills to radiation danger and DDT pollution. Science has suffered an immense loss of prestige and public trust from such careless prostitution of opinion to the demands of publicity. Furthermore, a lethal twice-mindedness pervades the whole arena of military and commercial research. Some powerful men in public science admit nuclear weapons and nuclear war will cause permanent genetic damage to all life, yet they work in government projects which produce such weapons and plan for such wars! Others admit that increasing carbon dioxide threatens our climate, yet they design engines spewing it into the atmosphere. Some agree that the earth has limited resources, yet assert that exploding populations can take care of themselves. The public, not knowing the worst, still knows enough to be sceptical, and while demanding that technology solve all our problems instantly on one hand, on the other is slower and slower to respond to scientific warnings of danger. While the blizzard of unreason muffles the impact of logic and alarm, the public goes floundering forward.

Scientists need to regain a species point of view. Decisions should be made from evidence, for humane risk and general survival. To do good and avoid evil was the first of Aquinas' rules of natural law under which science flourished, but this touchstone has been lost sight of in the rise of technology with its financial rewards. Also the public expects infinite technology to be developed merely by spending money on education and equipment, without understanding or prizing the paths, commitments and rigors of science.

The truth is not so easy. We have no way to mass-produce scientists. Before a student can acquire research potential he must consciously shed the conflicting dogmas of modern civilization. Authority and scientific method clash fatally and forever. On its own grounds science is just as serious, just as intolerant as Islam, Christianity or Marxism. One cannot pursue the method of science and also accept political limits to inquiry. No individual can be exempt from scrutiny, from chance of error. No belief can be spared the ordeal of testing, no conclusion the risk of refutation.

The options now placed before us by the scientific community are harsh. Already, popular myth-making, refuge in mysticism, drugs, and magic have made inroads on the rational response. But our huge populations now depend upon modern techniques of agriculture, transportation and energy production. Millions will die if these systems grind to a halt for any reason. We cannot go back to the land and find the abundance of early times, because that abundance has been consumed. Easily reached resources of coal, iron and oil are gone forever. We have used them up. The rich soil is spent. If something upset our present production, we would be without rescue. In this country this same impasse occurred once before.

The American Indians of the plains had been stable in numbers for years. They hunted on foot, food gathering, raising no crops until the Spanish came bringing horses. The horse captured from the Spanish changed the food balance of the plains Indian. On a horse he could outrun the buffalo. Growth of the central tribes began. Only two centuries later, the white hunters pressing west met a plains Indian culture completely adapted to the horse, completely centered upon the buffalo. At first the white man fought the Indian directly. But after a while he turned to something more deadly. He went after the buffalo herds instead. The white man had a newer weapon than the horse, he had the Henry and the Spencer rifles. We should doubt ourselves and acknowledge fear, for who could have foreseen a disaster so cruel, so complete for the flourishing tribes?

Within two short centuries buffalo-hunting had replaced food-gathering completely. The new technology supported a growth of population the old ways did not permit. The tribes transferred to a horse and buffalo technology. Surely the wisest Indians gathered in council looked upon this change of ways as progress, the coming of the horse as a goodness of the Great Spirit. Until disaster overtook them, they did not even imagine their danger. They had learned to count their wealth in horses but when the buffalo went, they starved. The horse could not help them.

We are in such a worldwide predicament today. Our technology has permitted every nation to expand. If technology were pulled from under us for any reason, as the white hunter pulled the buffalo from under the plains Indian, we could not survive in our expanded numbers. We also would starve as the Indians starved, or surrender as the Indians surrendered.

We cannot abandon science to the blizzard of unreason. We cannot abandon its stepchild, technology, either. Young people against the system will still have to take part in techniques of survival. Through the process of natural die-off and nonreplacement, the human mass can be returned to balance with environment and resources. We have to treat the temporary explosion of humans like the outbreak of any other overwhelming species. Wait for them to die. Clean up the dead. Set about restoring the overused and abused land. Prevent a recurrence. Science and technology offer us order, offer us control of this process.

At the peak of its external success the human experiment has come to a crisis of direction. We can stop here, unwilling to face the problem of human controls. The forces of tribal life will then carry us on. The environment will take its revenge. Our technology will have made it only more cruel, more terrifying, more complete.

Or we can try to apply to ourselves all we have learned, all we can logically predict. We will not control the ecosystem until we can regulate our own place in it: reduce our numbers and stretch out the timespan of our species. If the pleas are eloquent, control of ourselves can come as a sweeping response to these new ideas. Ecology and population control are modern forms of an old struggle, to free the minds and the bodies of men, to defend inquiry, and to insist on its vision of truth.

Today the very great antiquity of the distinction between African, Asian and Caucasian peoples is just beginning to be realized. New estimates place this divergence back before the ice age, before Cro-Magnon, before anything like civilization had arisen to pass on. By the time man lived in caves or used fire, there were at least three physical types widely distributed in separate areas of the world. There was certainly no single creation of modern man. Thus the antiquity of our difference, the overriding coherence of our likeness *is* important. These show us the direction evolution has refused to take for at least fifty thousand years. Time has failed to increase our separation. Long ago the main pressures of evolution turned from our body structures and became attached to the cultural and social arrangements we hand down to each other. In these arrangements we diverge. Many kinds of behavior have become natural to mankind.

Discoveries in this century suggest that man has not only been the prime killer of his animal enemies—saber-toothed tiger, lion, mastodon, buffalo—but also of his own competing races. With consummate skill he exterminated from the face of the earth many of his manlike cousins, his own primitive ancestors, not permitting them to survive into the present as less-adapted animals survived from the dim past. There are no Cro-Magnons, no Neanderthalensis, no Aurignacians—and why not, when there are baboons and chimpanzees? Probably we killed them, that is why not.

The dismay created by these discoveries is matched by horror of our own actions in this century. The mind leaps to Hiroshima and Dachau, to Biafrans in the Congo and Tatars in Russia, to the morass of Vietnam. We face ever-widening ripples of communal frictions from New York to Bombay to Singapore.

Man lost the myth of his divine creation in the last century. In this one, his myths of humanity are threatened. The great philosophers and humanists of the medieval church looked more accurately within themselves, for they declared that man by his reason could have a knowledge of goodness and justice, but man by that knowledge would not be prevented from committing evil. Choice between good and evil was regarded seriously. It was forced upon men then as now. Today, the strain of reason and the need for choosing are grim realities for a creature whose capacity to kill is as great as ours. To continue crowding ourselves together is asking for tragedy.

Therefore once again, reason and freedom of conscience are forcing the hand of authority. If it is natural to control death through science and medicine, it must be natural to control life. And to adopt measures, voluntary or coercive, to ensure species survival, is the most natural act of all.

The Species Point of View

22

THE RIM OF TWILIGHT sweeps over the surface of the earth and after it, lights flick on in milking barn and henhouse, in kitchens and theaters, and airports and city streets. The dark side of the earth gleams in the blank night. No other object in the planetary distance shows these odd patches and flashes of light, a light unstarlike, not of nature, disturbing in its uncertainty. For this faint glow there are no predictions, no table of motions, no entry in the sidereal almanac. The light glows from the regions of Perth, from the two coasts of North America, from Europe. The dark places are equally strange. There are stretches of darkness across Africa, across India, across the middle of the continents. What is the light? What is the dark?

Like a child running along in the meadow flashing his flashlight now up, now down the field, not so much lighting his own way as signaling in fear of the dark. "Here I am. See me!" Who comes running, breathless up the summer porch, "Did you see me down there? I signaled you. Did you see??"

The planet is signaling, using the light, but also sending it—where?

We believe that nobody sees, nobody near enough in light years to be part of our lifetime; nobody near enough to human shape to be part of our experience. Nothing from the outside is going to help us reach the species point of view about ourselves. Against Martians we might unite. Against the primitive destroyer within us, it is not certain that we are going to.

We can restore the ecological balance we have been so busily destroying only if we care enough. For us to care that much, we must believe that human life will continue, but for how long? This is an interesting conundrum. If changing our ways will buy only fifty or a hundred years, life might as well wag merrily on, callous, unequal, flamboyant and disintegrative. There would be little point in so short a purchase of time. But on what scale are we to become seriously interested by the prospect of added generations? Five hundred years, or five thousand? Or longer?

If we look forward to human use of the earth for five thousand years or more, the rationing problem becomes quite different from planning for five hundred. No matter what technology and energy resources may be developed in the future, a longer cruise is obliged to carry fewer people than a short one. We can get control of the rationing process by cutting our numbers nearly in half over the next hundred years. By eliminating conspicuous waste of all kinds we can stretch out that control into the future.

Human self-interest impels us to adopt the species rather than the tribal point of view because today our dangers are more serious than mere tribal clashes. They are atmospheric in the air we breathe, cellular in the food we eat. The pooled abilities of many races may be just enough to work out a human survival.

Human diversity increases the likelihood of species success in our checkerboard world. However pursuit of individual happiness is threatened by masses of other people, and is confined within sharp limits of oxygen and water, living space, and energy supply. We do not know what will be the limiting factor against which the species will bump with fatal suddenness. Formerly the strong tribe could rob the weak of food and water, but when oxygen is exhausted it is exhausted for weak and strong alike. When food or water is biologically poisoned, it is pointless to corner the supply.

Statements like these have become so common that they pass over us without touching a response, although the child sitting down to supper in America carries strontium-90 in his bones and DDT in his fat. No amount of anxious cherishing, nor disbelief will exempt him from these dangers. Today, love for children is tinged with dread, with what C. P. Snow calls "the darkness of the heart".

The best chance we have of human survival is not readily expressed in language, nor controlled by nations. It is not the property of the military nor the province of politics. It lies within the personal flesh, the personal lust, the personal loving. We have come to a time when deaths must catch up to births in order to rebalance people with resources. Only on the level of personal procreation can we expect to say no more shall be born until this dying time is passed.

No matter how reasonable it seems to protect the earth for future generations, and to avoid the suffering caused by over-births, we cannot count upon unscientific people to act upon scientific evidence. Science cannot change its facts to please their opinion. No amount of wishful thinking will make research successful. While uneducated people easily understand jobs, profits and political power, both here and abroad, the strict objectivity of science is understood by all too few. Thus, wherever a tradition of tribal self-interest has prevented a national or an international point of view, science may not prove adequate to impel population control. The scientific community may convince the United Nations and the United Nations may in turn convince its member-governments of obvious demographic facts. But to try to motivate common people by demographic argument is useless. They have to feel the need for fewer births in an immediate personal way.

Thus our fate will not be decided by majority vote nor anything like a plebiscite, but rather by winning over the most powerful, the most ethical imaginations of our time. The need must enter song and story, and the common understanding. Never was the Quaker maxim more important: "Speak truth to power!" But this truth must be made to reach down to levels of fear far below the conventional surface.

Young couples are readily influenced by the behavior of their own cohort and by the spoken needs of their society. This is why stopping at one or two children is a live option for community college and university students across America. In most of these places the small family is discussed. Powerful evidence pleads for it. Examples are being set.

The opposite situation exists for young couples not receiving higher education. At the present time many public schools are denied discussion. Financial or educational reward is not a motive for self-control among these young people. Thus we have a complex task ahead of us to rearrange social rewards. To defer first birth and to have only one or two children is a pattern which must have many kinds of reinforcing. For the poor it must pay and seem fortunate; for the ignorant it must be simple to achieve; for the natalist it must be convincing; for the rich and the proud, it must be fashionable and praiseworthy. The cohesive opinion of society favoring genuine reduction of population must affect all the types of people capable of reproducing. In this task there is work for everyone.

On the world scene it is doubtful if wars and famines and outbreaks of disease can be altogether prevented by a drop in births. The drop may not come fast enough. Yet those countries where education, and self-control are highly prized may be able to develop a balance between people and resources, just as families who are self-controlled have been able to do so. There are obvious limits to this option; even the most fortunate country is threatened by wars, poisons and pollutions beyond its borders.

The United Nations is struggling with the notion that there are rules of human life even governments must obey. It is struggling to bring to fruition the species point of view, to assert the values and rights of all nations and races, as well as of individuals.

Thus we are suddenly looking away from the consuming issues of the last three hundred years. Whether we like it or not, all forms of government will have to take very similar steps to reduce population and conserve their resources. It will matter less and less who owns the means of production, or how civil government is controlled. The ideology of both capitalism and communism currently gives priority to economics. The new ideology will give priority to ecology and species survival. In this new ideology, the traditions of both east and west will encounter common ground.

Today, scientists among us have clearly voiced our ecologic dangers, although calls to specific eco-action are not necessarily calls for an ethical change. We will be endangered by piecemeal efforts. Better quality of life hinges upon fewer people. Both require an ethical appeal. Only the full recognition of these new values can protect the ecosystem and lead us to new patterns of harmony.

The western style of population control will be vulnerable to aggressive natalist factions. Firm forms of restraint will have to be found within democratic countries for this type of group aggression. Nations able and willing to control their own population growth will also have to deal with the unchecked expansion of countries unable or unwilling to do so. Stupid overbreeding at home is not going to remain an acceptable reason for demanding emigration abroad. The United Nations will quickly recognize this. Valid objections to overbreeding should not be written off as racial prejudice. The outcome is too important to us all.

Today any nation which more than replaces itself is demanding an added share of the world's resources, whether its people emigrate or not. By this yardstick the United States is a major culprit in population pressure.

The American saga of exploitation and a rising standard of living once captured the imagination of the economic world, and especially of undeveloped nations. But its biological unlikelihood now strikes home with numbing force. Our story is a story the crowded world cannot repeat. It has many features of waste and ignorance no ecologist would want to repeat.

To protect what is left of the green breathing of the green lung from the inroads of technology will cause conflict among men, but not any serious moral dissension. A new pattern of smaller populations, of interaction rather than competition, will be the 20th century's answer to intolerance, to parochial religion, to private privateering and public repression of rights.

Recent political history was changed by Rousseau, Jefferson and Marx because they were part of an ethical revolt which touched off the felt needs of the people. Today the force seems spent which brought western civilization into modern times. Throughout two thousand years westerners migrated, carrying their laws and ideals of reason with them. Now that kind of expansion has ended.

Far from witnessing the end of European civilization we are only in the very opening chapters of its vindication and extension into the far corners of the world. The basic idea of the 18th century progressed not only as a struggle for freedom against government, but as a struggle between governments for independence. In this century, there have been crude military convulsions against the despotic regimes of the continent; Canada, Australia and the United States are forging ahead as governments of the people. Russia in its own way is now part of the European egalitarian thrust. The retreat of British, French and American empires appears to be a retreat of this civilization. But this is not so. These retreats result from conscious attitudes which accept short-term intervention but which recognize a contradiction between long-term interference and expressed beliefs. What is baffling to the Europeans who are the bearers of this civilization is the terrific velocity with which good and bad ideas have been adopted and have recoiled upon their originators, resulting in a casting-off of political and economic tutelage.

No government today can openly advocate, even if it openly pursues, a policy which fosters privilege at the expense of social justice. We have to detach ourselves a little from immediate crisis to perceive that the more hateful wars of this century are extensions into Asia of the essentially European conflict over privilege. Our antagonism and our partisanships are all part of the thrust of this great civilizing egalitarian ideal of the scientific centuries, which has by no means begun to implement itself or to come to an end.

There are many myths about the future, but only one reasonable mandate. The science-fiction myth offers the cold, massive, regulated world of 1984. This myth presupposes an endless increase of people, endless technologizing of our lives and our environment. Exploding populations of mankind will become specialized in fragile dependence upon central scientific authority. This is one extreme.

All the old myths of hell and damnation, of Kali and Armageddon, lie on the other extreme regarding with satisfaction the end of the human tale where demons and angels finally demolish between them the existence of men. These myths are equally opposed to rational curtailment of peoples. They lure the ignorant masses of mankind to accept ever-increasing disaster. They lead us toward a blizzard of unreason, where all effort at rational control is surrendered.

Between the myths of the past and the myths of the future lies the mandate for population control, control by ourselves for the sake of our children. If we are realistic, energetic and stubborn, remedies can be found. We must seek for them in a spirit of trial and error, and pragmatic hope.

The mandate to control and cut back our own populations lies well within the historical drift of European civilization. The notion of two children per couple, of one child per person is quite in keeping with its original ethical ideal. It is a completely consonant strand in the fabric of equal opportunity. Once we place the rationing of births in the perspective of all other rationings that are going on around us, we can take a more reasonable view of the future. Civilization is not going to settle for the myths of Armageddon nor for the myths of 1984, with ever-more cynical manipulation of humans. On the contrary, the future lies somewhere between these unlovely options. We will not give up easily the effort to find alternatives. For the next century, having one child or none is a pleasing alternative, and we should be ready to accept its necessity.

In earlier pages, we have seen madness in methods. We have seen the irrelevance of family planning. We have seen how easy it is to be twice-minded, and how it pervades our political and medical thinking. We have seen death control extending its hold on health care and research and charitable foundations. We have seen that man is selecting for drastic deselection in the human stock. We have felt the strange split between men and other animals in sexual behavior. We have sensed the lurking murderer in our tribal selves. Slowly emerging is the strange fact that excessive births endanger the very species they perpetuate.

In recent decades, projections of enormous population increase have dominated the media. In conference after conference, projections for increase become blueprints also. Governors, mayors, city managers, doctors' committees, bankers and road commissioners all plot the expanding course of future population, as well as their own expanding powers and budgets. In a status-ridden society, expansion adds to status. No one stops to ask the question of these people: Do we want all this growth? Will it be good for us? Who will enjoy it? Who will pay for it? The most important question of all is not even thought of. Why should we plan for growth that *will not occur?*

The human population is not going to continue to rise indefinitely. That is certain. Population will not climb the absurd curve proposed by the boosters of local economy or the prophets of highways. The prospects instead are for radical undulation, for a modified S-curve which comes about through drop in births or rise in deaths or both together. Nothing is standing still. We are heading toward a rapid resolution of the world crisis in fertility.

For a population undulating at the crest of its population density, there is nothing humane about intense short die-offs and over-births. For animal populations in this phase, die-off and replacement can remain unstable over an unknown number of oscillations as they do for the lemmings. Or a large initial drop in population can lead to more stable levels afterward. Final patterns of density are not yet set for human populations.

We make a mistake when we accept an upward curve of population as inevitable, for the fact is not here yet. We do not have to breed and build and plan for more millions. We can wake up at last to the vital part which pictures of our future play in the decisions of men. The up-curve must be disputed. A picture of a level population can break the grip of the up-curve on our social predictions, just as a right turn changes our picture of the road running straight into the future.

Once we have the notion of the turn approaching, the whole act of turning is simplified. Concentrating on the road beyond the turn, the imagined action translates into fact. We can turn the car, or we can stop at one or two, pursuing contraception, abortion and sterilization. When we have a clear image of the horizontal right-turn leveling-off of population, we can follow this image into action and population *will* level off.

The image is prior to the action. The image is prior to the will; the image is prior to all possibilities of wise decision.

This is the most important fact of all the population facts. Nothing overrides the power of human social imagination to produce social effects. If man imagines the control of fire, he will control fire. If he imagines disease control, he will control disease. If he imagines traveling in space, he will travel there. Once man imagines fewer people on a more joyous earth, he will produce fewer people and protect that earth.

Epilog

SOONER OR LATER population explosions in the animal kingdom
come to an end. Ecologic balance is reimposed from the outside as coercion or from the inside as instinct. As human creatures we may be less fortunate. We have more influence on our
options than animals. We can be played on by nightmares and
haunted by dreams. But we too will be finally coerced by the
ecosystem.

In the spring the swallows come without warning. Just then,
when they come, the first dancing columns of midges are seen
ascending in thermals from the sunshine. The food and the
feaster arrive together in a coercion we can hardly understand
for all our knowledge. The mixed flocks spend the summer and
suddenly, without dissent they are gone. The sweet chittering
falls silent. A band of finches or siskins sweeps through where
the swallows circled over the pond, and then the late Indian
summer insects have it all their own way at the end of the year.
Coerced by the larger ecosystem, the swallows leave, ready or
no, for long flights and distant valleys in Central and South
America. We, too, can go on a long migration into another
time.

Coerced by the larger ecosystem, the human imagination surveys the end of large-scale war, of country against country. It
surveys the fall of birth rates all over the world, and the slow
rise in share of land and cattle, of household goods and
nourishing food. From the air in winter the northern forests

used to smoke from thousands of fires burning over the logged-off acres. Now it is clear and still. The quality of timber which had become brittle and short-lived is slowly improving as the hills improve. Creeks run clean, water is caught in the sponge, floods and run-offs are checked high in the land. Slowly but surely, with the return of forests and the breakup of asphalt and cement, the deep springs are coming back.

One of the largest companies in America has spent thirty years removing unused pavement, sifting and restoring the soil and leasing out the land to young couples living nearby. The deserted gas stations, empty parking lots and dilapidated drive-ins turn into communal gardens, full of exuberant squash vines, and blazing zinnias, lettuce and dahlias and prize tomatoes. No plot is too small, no wasteland too polluted for the reclaimers. So greenery invades the urban scene.

Change, development and decay occur as before in city neighborhoods, but meanwhile the land is decorated with laughter and movement of people, giving some substance to the dream that all men can be brothers and lovers.

The notion of cost recedes before the notion of community, for the worker no longer pretends that the wage he is paid makes it right to endanger the green film.

Companies making millions of dollars in the new century are taxed on their energy-budgets; on the loss of vital resources which they use in production.

New ideals of sharing a livelihood jostle old ideals of making a fortune, for there is no price on the running and laughter of children, or the crumble of good earth between careworn fingers in the heart of what used to be the heartless city.

New skyscrapers exist, are even encouraged to save land and transportation, provided they are set back far enough to permit the free flow of air and sunlight. As an incentive to open space in the industrial centers of old towns, buildings are taxed according to the angle of sky they obscure from the center of the street. The nearer they come to the zenith, the more tax is piled on the upper stories, for even in the city, people are re-freshed by glancing upward at stars in the night sky.

The cities lose their look of ranked cement. The fronts of the new buildings are irregular and interesting. At least twenty per-cent of the new plot has to be in trees. The street has become again as it had been since early times, a meeting and a market-place, a place to loiter and observe, instead of an ugly tunnel to be hurried through. The depriving canyons of an earlier time are not repeated.

Mass markets flourish around the world. Large department stores and supermarkets are larger than ever. But instead of stilted show-windows shutting out the pavement and the peo-ple, the street floor is broken into by small shops like an Asian bazaar. Young craftsmen sell jewelry. Chefs cook special food. Girls sell embroidered fabric. There are public kilns and weav-ing rooms, places for tin-smithing, tiny dance floors and cafés. Meeting the crying need for something unique, something handmade and beautiful, a look of individuality returns to every-day life. Adaptive, romantic, crass and practical, the human society takes its new directions, encouraging its new crimes and its new successes.

The escape from death and from planetary disaster touches every face with the miraculous. Ceremony and festival acknowl-edge the balance between life and death. Neither in joy nor in desolation are individuals cut off from community life. Bells peal when the newborn is placed in the mother's arms. Hearing it, in celebration, the passers-by up and down the street ring small echoing bells which hang overhead on the street corners.

In the courtyard of death on the other side of the hospital a jet of continuous flame reflects in a pool of dark water. When the body of the dead comes into the hallway, policemen and helpers, nurses and by-standers pause, instead of pretending to hurry off about their business. Others take long torches from a rack beside the pool and light them in the flame. While the body of the dead is carried out they gather at the doorway.

Then one by one as the van draws away the torches are plunged like a salute into the dark water.

Births and deaths are in balance. Bells peal and flames are extinguished with equal frequency, for this is the condition of species survival. Gazing often and openly at mysterious death, the child grows up with a sense of intensified life, not ashamed to be grieved nor afraid to be joyful.

And so it happened. Like all cataclysms in the living record, no one knew where it began, where it would end, but the infestation had suddenly subsided. The curve of human population fell and was still falling.

The disappearance of one billion people from the face of the earth was hardly noticed while it was going on, so natural it seems for the old to die quietly when their time comes. The old died, and the young failed to replace them. The young generation were for peace, and they just quietly ceased to breed. "Poverty is a luxury we can't afford," they said. "The draft must go," they said. "There must be love in the world."

Of all the remedies proposed, the event was by far the strangest, the most spooky. A huge readjustment of peoples, one of the greatest of all time had silently taken place all over the globe. After the census was taken for the year 2030, suspicion became definite. The four billion people on earth together toward the end of the millennium had dropped below three billion in one generation. There were children, of course, but only the very old noticed that there were fewer of them. Then suddenly, the very old people also became few. The flood had passed. Where the human flood had been, green edges were springing up. In the green refuge, under a clearing sky, there would be children far, far into the future, but never again a human epidemic.

References

Chapter 2: Von Fritsch, Karl. *Dance Language of the Bees.* Cambridge: Harvard University Press, Belknap Press. 1967.

Chapter 3: Galton, Sir Francis. *Hereditary Genius.* Cleveland and New York: World Publishing Co. 1962.

Chapter 4: Petersen, William. *Population.* New York: Macmillan Co. 1961.

Chapter 5: Tinbergen, Nikko. *Curious Naturalists.* New York: Natural History Press. 1968.

Chapter 6: Calhoun, John. "Population Density and Social Pathology." *Scientific American,* February, 1962.
Chandrasekhar, Sripati. *Asia's Population Problem.* New York: Praeger. 1967.
Fabre, Jean Henri. *The Mason Bees.* Translated by Alexandre Texeira de Mattos. New York: Dodd Mead & Co. 1914.

Chapter 7: Brown, Harrison. *The Challenge of Man's Future.* New York: The Viking Press, Inc. 1954.
Buxbaum, Ralph and Mildred. *Basic Ecology.* Pittsburgh: The Boxwood Press. 1957.
Lack, David. *Darwin's Finches.* New York: Harper Brothers, Torchbooks. 1961.
Carson, Rachel. *Silent Spring.* Boston: Houghton Mifflin Co. 1962; *Under The Sea Wind.* New York: Simon & Schuster. 1941.
Hardy, Sir Alistair. *The Open Sea.* Vol. 1. The Plankton. Boston: Houghton Mifflin Co. 1956.
Peattie, Donald Culross. *Road of a Naturalist.* Boston: Houghton Mifflin Co. 1941.
White, Rev. Gilbert. *The Naturalist History of Selborne.* London: B. White and Sons. 1789.

Chapter 8: Andrewartha, H. G. *Introduction to the Study of Animal Populations.* Chicago: University of Chicago Press. 1961.
Dowdeswell, W. H. *Animal Ecology.* New York: Harper Brothers, Torchbooks. 1961.

Huxley, Julian. *Evolution: The Modern Synthesis.* New York: John Wiley & Sons. 1964.

Mayr, Ernst. *Animal Species and Evolution.* Cambridge: Harvard University Press. 1966.

Chapter 9: Dobzhansky, Theodosius. *Mankind Evolving.* New Haven: Yale University Press. 1962.

Roberts, D. F. and Harrison, G. A. *Natural Selection in Human Populations.* New York: Pergamon Press. 1959.

Mourant, A. E. *The Distribution of Human Blood Types.* Oxford, England: Blackwell. 1954.

Turnbull, Colin M. *The Forest People.* New York: Simon & Schuster. 1962.

Chapter 10: Zinsser, Hans. *Rats, Lice and History.* Boston: Little Brown & Co. 1934

Chapter 11: Defoe, Daniel. *A Journal of the Plague Year 1721.* New York: Signet, New American Library. 1960.

Snow, John. *Snow on Cholera.* London: Oxford University Press. 1936.

Chapter 12: Beals, Allan R. *Gopalpur: A South Indian Village.* New York: Holt, Rinehart & Winston. 1967.

Chaudhury, Nirad C. *Autobiography of an Unknown Indian.* Berkeley: University of California Press. 1968.

Mukerji, Dhan Gopal. *My Brother's Face.* New York: E. P. Dutton & Co. 1924.

Population Reference Bureau. "1969 World Population Data Sheet." Washington, D.C.

Chapter 14: Ardry, Robert. *African Genesis.* New York: Atheneum. 1961; *The Territorial Imperative.* New York: Atheneum. 1966.

Armstrong, Edward. *Bird Display and Behavior: An Introduction to the Study of Bird Psychology.* New York: Dover Publications. 1965.

Brown, Claude. *Manchild in the Promised Land.* New York: New American Library. 1965.

Lorenz, Konrad. *On Aggression.* Translated by M. K. Wilson. New York: Harcourt, Brace & World. 1966.

McKusick, Victor. *Foundations of Modern Genetics.* Englewood Cliffs, New Jersey: Prentice-Hall Foundations. 1965.

Chapter 16: Davis, Kingsley. "Population Policy: Will Current Programs Succeed?" *Science,* 158: 730. 1967.

Stycos, J. Mayone. *Human Fertility in Latin America*. Ithaca: Cornell University Press. 1968.

Chapter 18: Chermayeff, Serge and Alexander, Christopher. *Community and Privacy*. New York: Doubleday & Co., Anchor Books. 1965.

Doxiadis, Constantinos A. and Douglass, Truman B. *The New World of Urban Man*. Philadelphia: United Church Press. 1965.

Chapter 19: Fraiberg, Selma H. *The Magic Years*. New York: Scribner's Sons. 1959.

MacArthur, Robert H. "Population Ecology of Some Warblers of Northeastern Coniferous Forests." *Ecology* 39: 599-619. 1958.

Neill, A. S. *Summerhill*. New York: Hart Publishing Co. 1960.

Popper, Karl. *The Open Society and Its Enemies*. 5th ed. New York: Harper Brothers, Torchbooks. 1963.

Wiener, Norbert. *The Human Use of Human Beings*. Garden City, New York: Doubleday & Co., Anchor Books. 1954.

Chapter 20: Aquinas, St. Thomas. *The Summa Theologiae*, from *Introduction to Saint Thomas Aquinas*. Edited by A. C. Pegis. New York: Random House, Modern Library. 1948.

d'Entreves, A. P. *Natural Law*. London: Hutchinson & Co. 1951.

Feuerbach, Ludwig. *The Essence of Christianity*. Translated by George Eliot. New York: Harper Brothers, Torchbooks. 1957.

Chapter 21: Frazer, Sir James G. *The Golden Bough*. London: Macmillan Co. 1907.

Kierkegaard, Soren. *Fear and Trembling. The Sickness Unto Death*. Princeton: Princeton University Press. 1941.

Malraux, Andre. *Les Metamorphoses des Dieux*. Paris: La Galerie de La Pleiade. 1957.

Marx, Karl and Engels, Friedrich. *The German Ideology*. Edited by R. Pascal. New York: International Publishers. 1947.

Thompson, Sir D'Arcy Wentworth. *On Growth and Form*. Cambridge, England: University Press. 1942.

Tillich, Paul. *The Courage To Be*. New Haven: Yale University Press. 1952.

Wilson, E. B. *The Cell in Development and Inheritance*. New York: Macmillan Co. 1925.

Wittfogel, Karl. *Oriental Despotism*. New Haven: Yale University Press. 1957.

Wittgenstein, Ludwig. *Philosophical Investigations*. New York: Macmillan Co. 1953.

INDEX